◆ PICKING MUTUAL FUNDS FOR EVERY LIFE STAGE

Junius Ellis
and the Editors of MONEY

Other MONEY Books by Junius Ellis

♦ *Making the Most of Your Money Now*

♦ *Your Best Money Moves Now*

♦ *Guide to a Secure Retirement*

♦ *Winning with Mutual Funds*

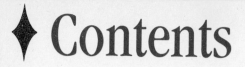

♦ Contents

To order MONEY Magazine, call Customer Service at 800-633-9970
or write to MONEY, P.O. Box 60001, Tampa, Florida 33660-0001.

Picking Mutual Funds for Every Life Stage

Editor: Junius Ellis
Designer: Laura Ierardi, LCI Design
Cover: Photo by Walter Hodges

◆ Foreword

Investing For a Lifetime

Many Americans are conditioned from child-hood to expect their standards of living to rise as their lives and careers progress. If you are in your forties or fifties, however, you could be stunned to discover when you add up your net worth that you already have amassed quite a bundle. Even if you're just starting a family, you could be sur-prised at your potential for accumulating serious money. According to government surveys, some 850,000 people had built up estates worth at least $500,000, and half a million had socked away more than $250,000. Whether you aspire to or have attained such affluence, the chal-lenge confronting you is to keep those assets growing without taking unacceptable risks.

The solution for more and more people is mutual funds, which in the 1990s have been as profitable in practice as they are sensible in theory. By pooling small investors' money to buy and sell securities on their behalf, a mutual fund provides many of the advantages once available only to the wealthy. These include professional management, diversified holdings and ready access to your cash, all at a reasonable price. For these services some funds impose a sales charge, or load, on top of annual management fees and operating expenses that average just 1.4% of stock funds' assets and 0.8% of bond funds' assets. The payoff? Over a recent three-year period, stock funds as a group returned a tidy 10% annually (assuming reinvestment of dividends in additional fund shares). Even seemingly stodgy U.S. Treasury bond funds rewarded holders with three-year returns averaging 6% annually, nearly double the 3.5% earned by riskless three-month U.S. Treasury bills (the equivalent of cash for fund managers).

The rising popularity and strong performance of funds come fortuitously at a time when many of us face difficult financial issues ahead, including continued job insecurity, reduced health care benefits and an aging Social Security safety net. Let's face it. The days when employers and the government provided financial security to the grave are history. These days you have to rely primarily on yourself to make sure that your family's future is adequately provided for. The question no longer is if but when and how aggressively you need to get started as an investor.

The objective of this book is to answer such questions, as precisely as possible, so that you can be successful with mutual funds regardless of your experience or goals as an investor. Start by rating yourself as a fund-holder using the quiz "What's Your Investing IQ" on page 8. Then we supply you with model fund portfolios (see Chapter 1) that can be tailored to various stages of your financial life. Along the way we provide concise explanations and insights that will assist you in developing a strategy to achieve your goals, be they capital growth, income or a combination of the two. Then we'll teach you how to select funds that will help you reach those milestones without subjecting you to added risk. We also give tips on choosing the best fund family to call your own; minimizing fund expenses so that profits go into your pocket rather than the purveyors'; deciding when to sell your fund shares; and deploying your portfolio of funds so that you keep more of your gains out of the clutches of the tax man.

Don't worry if you stumble over an unfamiliar term or strategy. Turn instead to our glossary at the end of the book. Indeed, this volume strives to answer just about every question you might have about funds including three very common ones facing investors today.

When's the right time to invest? Whether the market is headed up or down, many investors' biggest fear is getting in at the wrong time. The truth, incredible as it seems, is that there's no wrong time as long as you select an appropriate fund or mix of funds and buy in gradually. Consider the following. Suppose that 20 years ago you set up a $5,000 per annum investing program in Standard & Poor's 500-stock index. Assume further that in every one of those 20 years you had the uncanny bad luck to invest that stake on the very day the index hit its annual high. For fun, the American Funds group in Los Angeles calculated the anticipated carnage of such mistiming. Well, that hapless investor ended up with a huge profit on a portfolio worth over $460,000. That works out to an annual return of 13.6%, just below the 14.3% for the S&P 500 index itself (assuming you put in $5,000 at the beginning of each of the 20 years). The fact is, there's no profit in, or prayer of, trying to time the market. The ideal moment to buy is when the market is hitting terrifying new daily lows and everyone else is desperate to sell. Nobody really knows how low is low. No trumpet blows when the turnaround is nigh. The one certainty is that when a bull market does come, it comes in a fevered rush, a day here, a week there.

Why shouldn't I play it safe? A study by statistician Ned Davis tested the premise that the real peril is not being in the market but being out of it at the wrong time. An individual who had bought the S&P 500 index in January 1980 and held it during the decade that fol-

What's Your Investing IQ?

Anyone who keeps up with financial matters and markets should have no trouble with these queries. Score 10 points for each correct answer, explained on the right.

1. You can't lose money investing in a U.S. Treasury bond because it is backed by the United States Government. True or false?

2. Investing in a mutual fund that holds a diversified portfolio of stocks protects your investment against market declines. True or false?

3. You meet a financial planner whose business card says that he or she is a Registered Investment Adviser. This means the planner
a) meets rigorous standards set by the SEC
b) is recommended by the SEC
c) has simply paid a $150 registration fee to the SEC

4. You're considering investing in a mutual fund that's expected to distribute $1 a share in dividends. You should
a) buy now so you'll get the distribution
b) buy after the distribution is paid
c) buy either way, because it doesn't matter

5. You own a stock fund whose holdings loosely mirror the Standard & Poor's 500-stock index's recent price-earnings ratio of 19 and dividend yield of 2.8%. This means that the fund is
a) undervalued by historical standards
b) mildly overvalued
c) fairly valued

6. You put $1,000 in a stock fund two years ago. The fund's trading price declined 40% the first year and rose 40% the next. As a result, you've
a) lost money
b) made money
c) broken even

7. You own bonds maturing in five years that are likely to be called, or redeemed, as early as next year. The best gauge of your return is their
a) current yield
b) yield to maturity
c) yield to call

8. You own shares in the Germany Fund. The value of your fund's investment in U.S. dollars would be higher if
a) the dollar weakens against the Deutsche mark
b) the dollar strengthens against it
c) neither; a change in the dollar's value doesn't matter in this case

9. The figure that best reflects a mutual fund's performance is
a) its current yield
b) the total of dividends and capital gains it has paid
c) its total return

10. If interest rates climb one percentage point, which of these securities would be hurt the least?
a) a 20-year zero-coupon bond
b) a 20-year bond selling at its face value
c) a 20-year bond selling at a premium above its face value

Answers:
1. False. If interest rates rise, the market value of all bonds falls. **2.** False. A portfolio holding stocks alone cushions only against losses in specific stocks. **3.** c. Virtually anyone can register with the SEC as an investment adviser; no professional credentials are required. **4.** b. By waiting, you'll avoid taxes on the distribution. **5.** b. Stocks are generally considered overvalued when the market's price-earnings ratio is around 20 or higher and its dividend yield is lower than 3%. **6.** a. To make up your loss, you would need a 67% gain. **7.** c. The yield to call reflects both the shortened stream of interest payments and the faster principal repayment (sometimes more than the bond's face value) that occurs when a bond is redeemed early. **8.** a. The portfolio is valued in Deutsche marks. If it is converted to a dollar value, the stronger Deutsche mark will buy more dollars, thus increasing your return. **9.** c. Total return includes all income and capital gains distributions plus the change in the fund's share price. **10.** c. The lower a bond's coupon rate and the longer the maturity, the more its price fluctuates with interest rates. A zero has no coupon rate, and a premium bond has a higher coupon rate than one selling at face value. Thus the premium bond would be hurt least.

Scoring:
100: Congratulations! You could be the next fund phenom. 70 to 90: You've mastered the basics. 50 to 60: Bone up before making any big investments. 40 or lower: It's time to start learning about investing.

lowed would have annual gains averaging almost 18%. But if you had missed just the 10 biggest market days of those 120 months, your average gain would have been cut to 13% a year. And if you had the misfortune to be out of the market during the 20 biggest days of the decade, your return would shrink to an annual 9%.

Do I know enough to take the plunge? Here's a quick review of the basics, whether you're a new investor or a seasoned veteran. A mutual fund is a corporation whose sole business is to pool money from investors like you and invest it in stocks, bonds, money-market instruments or some combination of the three. When you invest in a fund, you receive shares that represent part ownership of the fund's holdings and entitle you to a proportionate slice of whatever income and profits (or losses) those assets generate over a specified period of time. By joining forces with other investors, you enjoy a number of advantages over the do-it-your-selfers who venture into the securities markets on their own. Among the most important:

✦ Affordable professional management. You normally couldn't interest a professional money manager in minding your savings unless you had at least a six-figure sum to invest. With funds, however, you usually can get in the door for $1,000 to $3,000. Every fund has its own investment management team. These pros work full time tracking the markets, monitoring the fund's investments and deciding what and when to buy or sell. In exchange, the management team typically takes 0.5% to 1.5% of the fund's assets each year as an advisory fee. (For advice on evaluating various types of fund fees, see Chapter 5.)

✦ Ample diversification. Stock funds own shares in about 90 companies, on average, while bond funds hold 70 issues. By investing in such a large number and wide range of securities, funds virtually eliminate the risk that an unforeseen plunge in the price of a single stock or bond could take a big chunk out of your money.

How Peter Lynch Picks Winning Funds

Peter Lynch left behind the best record in the mutual fund industry's history when he retired in 1990 at age 46 from the helm of Fidelity Magellan, the country's largest at $33 billion in total assets. From 1977, when he took over the fund, to his retirement, Magellan appreciated an incredible 2,800%. That works out to almost 30% annually, or double the S&P 500 index's return over the corresponding period. How did Lynch accomplish such a feat? More than any other manager, he was able to anticipate the types of companies whose fortunes were improving. "I kept an open mind," he says. "Some managers are limited to, say, growth stocks. But I could and did buy gas utilities, railroads, steel companies, turnaround savings and loan institutions." In retirement, Lynch has written two best-selling books and sits on the investment committees of Boston College, his alma mater, and eight charities, helping these organizations to choose money managers for their endowment funds (a process that's similar to selecting funds for a portfolio). Lynch's advice to mutual fund investors:

✦ "Nobody who needs their money in one to two years should be in stocks or stock funds. But if you have a long investment horizon, a well-selected portfolio of stock funds is bound to prove a winner."

✦ "No manager or type of fund will succeed in all seasons. But if you buy one or two funds in different categories, you should have at least one all-star in any kind of market. The five categories I'd recommend are aggressive growth funds, which buy any and all kinds of stocks; emerging growth funds, which seek fast-growing smaller companies; large-company growth funds, which search for established companies increasing their earnings 15% a year or better; value funds that hunt for firms where undervalued assets, not current earnings, are the main attraction; and special-situations funds, which buy companies where something unique (like the possibility of a takeover) could change their prospects."

✦ "Don't try to change your portfolio frequently. But for new investments, consider choosing a fund style if it has been lagging for a long time. Right now, that would be large-company growth funds, which have trailed value-oriented funds for several years."

✦ Access to your cash. Most mutual funds are open-ended. That means they, unlike conventional corporations, don't issue a set number of shares that trade on the stock markets or over the counter. Instead, open-ended funds issue new shares whenever you invest and buy them back whenever you cash in. Thus when you want to buy or sell, you don't have to find another investor to take the other side of the deal. That's a big plus if you invest in markets where securities trade infrequently, such as certain small-company stocks or municipal bonds.

✦ An array of options. If the securities in the fund's portfolio appreciate, the value of your shares rises commensurately. If you redeem your shares at the higher price, you score a capital gain. You also net a gain if your fund sells some of the securities in its portfolio at a profit. Funds typically pay out all the year's net trading profits in a single capital gains distribution, usually in December. And if your fund owns bonds or other interest-bearing securities or stocks that pay dividends, the fund will also pay that income to you in the form of monthly, quarterly or semi-annual income distributions. You can elect to have either kind of distribution paid to you in cash, which you might choose to do if you plan to live off the income. But if you're investing to build your wealth, you should order the fund to reinvest the distributions in additional shares. It can make a huge difference. Say you invested a $10,000 sum 13 years ago with Peter Lynch, then manager of the famed Fidelity Magellan fund (see page 11 for his investment tips). And say you chose to receive dividends and capital gains in cash. At last count, you would have received about $23,750 in payouts and your stake in the fund would have grown to roughly $23,500. If, on the other hand, you had reinvested your dividends and gains in the fund, you would have shares worth nearly $104,000.

Let's hope this last anecdote settles the issue of when to get started. Today is better than tomorrow. Yesterday would have been better than either. But then, yesterday you didn't have this book. So read on. And good luck.

◆ One

Profiting Through Life's Passages

F resh out of college, Deborah Clary took her future into her own hands and became an investor. The office manager for a Columbia, S.C. financial planning firm, Clary had absorbed enough theory around the water cooler to know that stocks were the best choice for an unmarried recent grad whose most immediate financial objective, the down payment for a house, was five to 10 years off. But beyond that, she was a neophyte. "I knew just enough to know that I didn't know enough to run out and buy stocks myself," she explains. So Clary, like millions of first-time investors, bought funds (see "A Beginner Sets Her Sights on a Cool Million" later in this chapter). True, she had the advantage of working with pros. But that's not a prerequisite for success. To get started, you need an understanding of your financial goals, tolerance of risk and resolve to size up funds. For examples of how to mix funds to fit the financial profiles of different types of investors, check out the allocation charts in "Smart Portfolios for Every Stage of Your Life" beginning on page 17.

Investors increasingly view diversification as their silver bullet, the one terminator to every threat. By dividing your money among a variety of complementary funds, you can reduce your risk and maintain (or even enhance) your return. Achieving the optimum combination, however, is not as simple as dialing an 800 number. The passages in your life bring changes in the degree of diversification that you require as well as subtle shifts in your portfolio itself. No matter what your age is or how you apportion your assets, keep in mind that the best way to stay diversified is to formulate a strategy you will not feel trapped by later. The key is to find your comfort zone—and to know it may change as you progress through your life and career.

Starting out. A lifetime plan for building wealth and conquering risk begins when you first accumulate assets in your name, usually in your twenties. At that time you should diversify broadly in various categories of funds. Since you have plenty of time to ride out losses at this stage, you can afford to take somewhat greater risks than you would later in life. Therefore, your biggest bets should be in three types of stock funds focused, respectively, on large, established firms, smaller companies and those based overseas (each is discussed in detail in Chapter 2). As for bonds, funds that own corporate, U.S. government or municipal issues with intermediate terms (maturing in 10 years or fewer) provide the most generous combination of yield and possible appreciation.

Getting married. You may have a well-balanced portfolio for a single person. But what do you do if your newly betrothed loves racy sector funds (also discussed in Chapter 2) invested solely in, say, technology stocks? The solution seems easy enough. You simply add up your combined assets and then reallocate them according to a mutually acceptable plan. In fact, the process often entails a fair amount of soul searching. You should think hard, for instance, before eliminating a category of volatile investments just because one party feels skittish about it. But keep in mind that both owners of a portfolio should be comfortable—and vigilant for potential land mines. Prominent among them is the increasingly common case of a two-career couple whose jobs are in the same field or even company. If they have been contributing regularly to their firms' stock-purchase plans, they both are doubly vulnerable to a cyclical downturn in the industry's profitability and payroll. Thus the couple should sell some shares, and reinvest the proceeds in a diversified fund, even if they're bet-the-farm bullish on their company's prospects.

Raising a family. Because your kids could become your biggest expense, each birth is likely to cause you to reconsider just how your wealth is divvied up. But the event shouldn't occasion a wholesale rejiggering. Instead, let your holdings ride while you try to meet short-term needs by extracting cash from money-market funds. Remember too that the amount you put aside for college is part of your total portfolio and not some segregated sector of it, even if the money is in your child's name. If you decide to load your kids' college account with growth-minded stock funds, for instance, you may need to lighten up on such funds in your portfolio as a whole. Be aware as well of when you will need to tap the savings. You should gradually reduce your holdings of stock funds as you approach those tuition bills. That way you won't get caught having to cash in during a sudden slump in the market.

Changing jobs. When you leave yours, you may have trouble keeping your portfolio properly poised. For example, you may receive a lump sum from a company-sponsored savings plan and will need to decide how to allocate it. The best strategy depends mostly on the circumstances of your leave-taking. If you are moving directly to another job at comparable pay, you may simply want to roll the money over into a self-directed IRA (Individual Retirement Account) and rebalance your other holdings as needed. If you expect to be out of work for a while, however, resist the immediate temptation to disrupt your portfolio mix by weeding out the riskier holdings and bulking up on cash. A short-term disruption shouldn't upset a long-term plan. If you have an emergency fund equal to three months or more of expenses, you can probably ride out the episode without being forced to sell long-term holdings such as stock funds.

Splitting up. While divorce is often messy, disengaging your investments shouldn't be. That's because stockbrokers and mutual fund sponsors generally are willing to reissue jointly registered fund shares in separate names. The exception, of course, is real estate. Whatever you both own may have to be sold and divided, thus adding the task of integrating the proceeds into your own portfolio. Now is the perfect time to reassess whether you are comfortable owning singly what you invested in jointly only a while ago. Once you have determined that, you may still need to reallocate your portfolio (just as you may when a spouse dies). If you were depending on someone else's income as well as your own, you may want to shift a small percentage of growth-oriented assets, such as small-company stock funds, into income-generating bond funds (see Chapter 3).

Calling it quits. Once you reach your sixties, which will probably be the decade you retire, many of your financial problems will be behind you. Your children, if any, may be grown and even out of the house. Your home may be largely paid off. And you may be on the verge of making the classic mistake of unloading stock funds in a quest for greater income and capital preservation, thereby leaving yourself vulnerable to the risk of rising inflation. Assuming that inflation stays at around 3% annually, for example, it would cut the purchasing power of today's dollar in half in only 12 years. Thus you should still pursue growth via a 40% stake in stock funds. The rest of your porftolio should be stashed in sturdy, interest-paying bond funds and money-market funds.

Smart Portfolios for Every Stage of Your Life

♦ YOUNG ACHIEVER

Single Woman, Age 25 - Investment: $10,000

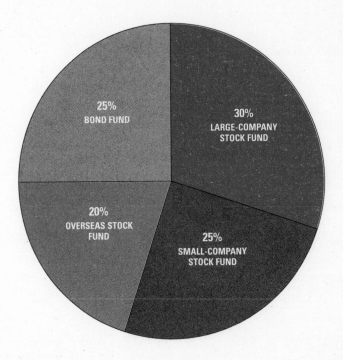

25%
BOND FUND

30%
LARGE-COMPANY
STOCK FUND

20%
OVERSEAS STOCK
FUND

25%
SMALL-COMPANY
STOCK FUND

With a long way to go before retirement, she can take the necessary risks
to gun for high returns. Three stock funds diversified among large and
small U.S. companies plus foreign shares do that work, while a single
bond fund hedges against stock market declines. Four funds should be
a maximum. Any more would stretch her limited resources too much.

◆ Nest Builders

Married Couple, Mid-Thirties, Two Preschoolers - Investment: $50,000

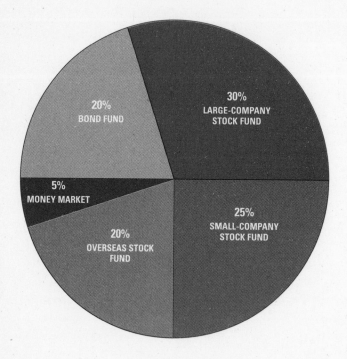

30%
LARGE-COMPANY
STOCK FUND

20%
BOND FUND

5%
MONEY MARKET

25%
SMALL-COMPANY
STOCK FUND

20%
OVERSEAS STOCK
FUND

The children's eventual college bills add one more long-term expense to this family's financial picture, making high returns a must. Thus 75% of their assets should go into stock funds, including a 25% slice in small-company funds. Depending on the couple's federal tax bracket, up to half of their bond investment should be in tax-free municipal bond funds.

♦ Peak Earners

Married Couple, Early Fifties, Three Teenagers - Investment: $250,000

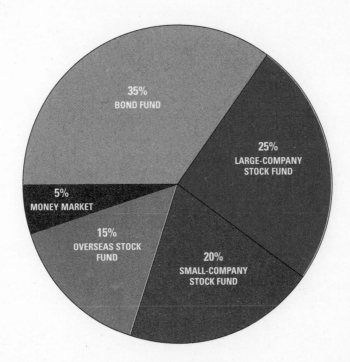

We assume that about 60% of this couple's portfolio is already earmarked for their retirement. That portion should go entirely into U.S. and overseas stock funds that are invested for capital growth. Most of the remaining money should be stashed in relatively stable, income-generating bond funds targeted to pay for their kids' current and coming college bills.

Smart Portfolios for Every Stage of Your Life

♦ THE ENJOYERS

Married Couple, Early Sixties, Two Grown Children - Investment: $350,000

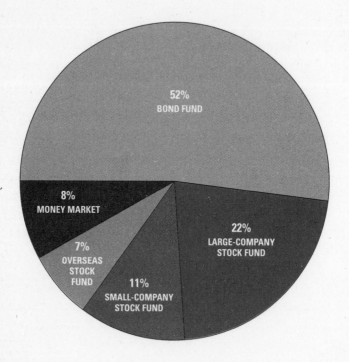

Their main goals are to conserve principal and generate income to live on. Accordingly, 60% of their assets goes into bond funds and money-market funds. To help keep pace with inflation during retirement, however, the couple still need to be invested in stock funds. Indeed, we would recommend a nearly 20% stake in fairly volatile small-cap and overseas funds.

Five Key Questions to Address

It's easy to describe the perfect fund. It offers stellar long-term gains, bountiful dividends and never, ever loses money. Alas, such a paragon doesn't exist. No fund can deliver both high returns and safety. Investing always means weighing potential benefits against risks. The cardinal rule: the more safety you demand, the less return you can expect, and vice versa. That means you cannot search intelligently for the best funds without some soul searching first. These questions will help you define what's best for you.

Do you need growth, income or safety? You're a growth investor if your key need is to build capital for a major future expense that's five or more years away, such as your kids' college education or your own retirement. The best funds for you invest mainly for capital appreciation. Such funds have a strong record of appreciation over long periods but are also the most prone to harsh short-term setbacks. As a result, you shouldn't consider yourself a growth investor unless you can endure painful stretches when your fund is down 20% or more. If you want your funds to help you pay ongoing expenses, such as your living costs in retirement, you're an income investor. Look at funds invested partly in bonds and sporting above-average yields. If you need money for an expense you will incur within a few years, what you need from your funds is safety. Your best choices are ultrasafe money-market funds. The drawback is that their yields have been achingly low in recent years.

How much risk can you handle? Think of risk as the entry fee you pay to invest. You can choose to take a lot or a little, but you can never avoid it entirely. The payback for assuming risk is potential return. The most aggressive stock funds, for example, have suffered precipitous falls of 20% or so in their worst years. But their long-term returns, which lately averaged 12% annually, make a compelling case for investing in them anyway. "Stocks almost always

A Beginner Sets Her Sights on a Cool Million

Deborah Clary knew absolutely zip about mutual funds when she was hired as office manager for J.E. Wilson Advisors, a Columbia, S.C. financial planning firm, several years ago. She had just earned her B.A. in media arts at the University of South Carolina and had received as a graduation gift from her dad a $6,000 money-market account. "I'd never really paid attention to investing before," explains Clary, 23. Then she heard a TV commercial telling how a 23-year-old investor who begins saving $150 a month could possibly retire a millionaire. "That raised my eyebrows," she recalls. "I figured I'd better get started!"

Saving for a house to call her own. Clary first defined her biggest financial goal, which is to save enough for a house down payment within five to 10 years, and started learning about stock and bond funds by talking to her firm's professionals. "I knew funds could provide the diversity and security I need," she says. She favored no-loads ("I want my money working for me, not padding someone else's pocket") and put $1,000 into Janus Fund, a growth portfolio, after reviewing the prospectus and noting its high rating and below-average risk by fund ranker Morningstar.

Balancing the risks of stock funds. Clary put another $3,000 into Vanguard's Wellesley Income Fund, which was invested 63% in bonds and 37% in stocks. This decision was influenced by a chart compiled by Ibbotson Associates, an investment analysis firm. "It illustrated that adding bonds to a stock portfolio can actually increase your return while reducing your risk," says Clary. Reinvesting her dividends made her think of Wellesley Income as a growth fund. And soon after, she began socking away another $50 a month in both Janus and Wellesley Income, using an automatic bank deduction plan.

The small-company edge. By then she had learned of the historic advantages of small-company funds and put the remaining $2,000 into one noted for its low volatility, Pennsylvania Mutual. "I liked the manager's approach of finding undervalued stocks," she says. As for monitoring her portfolio, Clary says: "I don't check my funds' daily performances. But if I see that one had a big drop or that a manager is leaving, then I'll watch it more closely." With such an early start, she figures she might just be able to retire early, move to the coast of South Carolina and pursue her favorite sport, scuba diving. "I've seen a lot of our clients who don't earn that much made wealthy by steady saving," beams Clary.

beat bonds in the long run," says Ken Gregory of the newsletter *No-Load Fund Analyst.* "This has been true for most of this century despite wars, economic crises and global change." Thus risk isn't necessarily bad as long as you don't take on more than you can handle.

When will you need your money? As a rule, the longer you're planning to hold on to your fund shares, the more you can afford to shoot for the stock market's higher returns. Say you had invested in the S&P 500 index at the start of any calendar year in the past 55 years and pulled out after 12 months. According to the research firm Ibbotson Associates in Chicago, you would have made money two out of three times. Had you held on for five years, your odds of making a profit would have improved to four out of five. And if you stood by your stocks for 10 years, you would have finished in the black 96% of the time.

How much could you bear to lose? No matter how impressive a fund's long-term record may be, you won't score big if you bail out when the fund turns temporarily cold. So ask yourself how much you could stand to see your investment plunge in a given year before pulling the ripcord. Bailard Biehl & Kaiser, an investment and financial planning outfit in San Mateo, Calif., uses the following rough-and-ready gauge of risk tolerance. If you're willing to stomach losses of 10% or more in a year, you're an aggressive investor. That suits you for high-risk, high-return funds such as those invested for aggressive growth or in small-company stocks. A 5% threshold of pain suggests you're interested in trading off some performance for safety in, say, total return funds that blend yield-rich stocks and bonds. If you're unwilling to tolerate any losses, you're too conservative for virtually any stock fund and all but the safest bond portfolios. Your options are money-market funds or those invested in government bonds of short or intermediate maturities.

How much advice do you need? Funds can be sold in either of two ways. Many funds are peddled by stock-

brokers, independent planners and insurance agents. You get the salesperson's advice in choosing your fund. But the fund will deduct a commission (the load) from your investment either in an up-front fee of 4% to 8.5% or in some combination of redemption charges and ongoing annual charges. No-loads are sold by fund sponsors directly to investors without commission. The money usually changes hands by mail or by bank wire, though big outfits like Fidelity and Dreyfus have walk-in offices in many cities. Note, however, that not all no-loads are free of commissions. For example, about a third of Fidelity's directly sold funds carry so-called low loads of 2% to 3%, which the company itself pockets. The low load isn't as onerous as the charges levied by broker-sold funds, but then you don't get any advice for your money either.

For every load fund on the market, you can almost always find an equally promising no-load. Don't believe a fund salesperson who tells you that load funds have an innate advantage because they can afford to hire better stock pickers or because their annual expenses are lower. Neither is necessarily true. There's no difference in performance between load and no-load funds. So whether to go load or no-load hinges on how much you value a salesperson's fund-picking prowess and ongoing advice.

 ## Find Funds to Fit Your Profile

The word portfolio conjures images of artists carrying samples of their best work that have been methodically chosen, updated and arranged for maximum effect. Savvy investors take the same kind of care assembling a fund portfolio, selecting funds not only for their particular promise but also for how well they complement the other funds in the portfolio. The result, when you do it right, is a kind of investing alchemy. Your portfolio overall becomes less risky than the sum of its individual components without a corresponding drop in return.

Such thoughtful portfolio design has paid off for Bruce and Gari Ann Douglass of Burbank, Calif. They started investing in the late 1980s soon after Gari Ann changed jobs and rolled over $50,000 from a 401(k) savings plan into an IRA. That $50,000 has swelled to $80,000 in their varied portfolio of funds. Every month they shift a set amount from money funds, where they've parked cash, into stock and bond funds in the same families. When the market is down, they move more (see "Mr. Mom's Recipe Is Heavy on Diversification" on the next page). You don't have to have $50,000 or dozens of funds to make your assets work together in a portfolio. You can start with as little as $1,000 and a single fund. What you do need are clear financial goals and a basic understanding of how to build a sturdy portfolio.

Diversify for balance and risk reduction. If fund investing were a form of meditation, there would be no mistaking its mantra—diversify, diversify, diversify. The practice of offsetting one investment's vulnerabilities with another's strengths is the principal ingredient in a well-constructed portfolio. It's what curbs risk without canceling growth. Think of it as a way of hedging your bets. Individual funds, of course, are inherently diversified. But owning a bunch of stocks does you little good when the whole market plunges. So you want your portfolio to include funds that embrace a wide variety of assets. The key is to mix and match funds invested in markets that are not correlated (that is, go up and down at different times). Most experts agree that your fund portfolio should include the three main assets—stocks, bonds and cash.

✦ Stocks are the engines of capital growth, promising inflation-beating long-term gains, but they're also subject to the greatest short-term market swings.

✦ Bonds are useless against the insidious advance of inflation, but they normally prosper when the economy is weak and stocks are falling.

✦ Cash, a catchall for money-market securities and short-term bonds, is essentially inert. It barely keeps up

Mr. Mom's Recipe Is Heavy on Diversification

Bruce Douglass, 43, is a stay-at-home dad who cares for his and wife Gari Ann's two young sons, cooks the family meals and keeps his six rules of investing on the refrigerator door. The first asserts: "No one will take better care of your money than you will."

Juggling family and funds. Bruce took over the family finances in 1988 after quitting his bank manager job to tend their firstborn. Since Gari Ann, 34, was earning more as an accountant for Columbia Pictures, the couple had calculated how much of his salary would be left after taxes, day care and the like. "We realized that I'd be left with only a month of real income after working my tail off to pay someone else to raise our son," he says. "So I became Mr. Mom." Soon after that, Gari Ann was raided away by MCA Pictures and received $62,000 in stock and 401(k) distributions from Columbia. "I had the choice of managing it myself or hiring someone else," explains Bruce. "I opted to try myself."

Homegrown asset allocation. He rolled over what he could into an IRA and spent the next two years devising on his home computer his own plans for asset allocation and dollar cost averaging (described in detail in this chapter). "If I don't get greedy," he says of his gradual escalation into stock funds, "I won't get burned." At last count, the Douglasses owned a portfolio worth about $80,000 invested in an incredible 30 funds. Isn't that taking diversification too far? Bruce defends his approach even though he concedes that it violates his refrigerator rule No. 6 ("Keep it simple, stupid"). Says he: "If I think stocks are rising too quickly, I can make a phone call and move into more conservative funds without losing my shirt." Still, he rejects market timing and limits his fund switches to two a year.

Gourmet food and Scottish frugality. Gari Ann credits Bruce "with allowing me to really advance in my profession" (she has moved up to controller of Paramount Pictures' home video division). In fact, she maintains that his gourmet cooking and "Scottish frugality" have made him a better homemaker than she could have been. And she adds: "He has done an outstanding job managing the portfolio; he really throws himself into it." Every Friday night after putting the boys to bed, the couple relaxes by watching TV's *Wall Street Week* and updating their funds' performances on a spreadsheet. "So much for romantic Friday nights," she laughs. Otherwise, Bruce spends most of his time on the boys. "They are so active," he says. "I can't do much of anything that doesn't involve them."

with the relentless march of inflation. But cash holds its value when both stocks and bonds slip.

Match your fund portfolio to your goals. This process, the heart of managing a portfolio, starts with a simple question. What's the money for? Is it for retirement in 20 years or a new car next year? If you're sure you won't need the money for five to 10 years, you should tilt your portfolio toward stocks, the assets that provide the best long-term return, and ignore the inevitable market ups and downs in the meantime. If you expect to need the cash in five years or less, you'll have to play it safer by putting a larger share of your money in bonds and cash.

You'll also want to consider how much income you rely on from your investments. The more cash flow you require, the more you should tilt your portfolio toward bond funds or to income-producing stock funds. But you'll first need to square that advice with your own internal risk meter. Often there's a wide gap between what makes sense financially and what people feel comfortable with emotionally. Many investors can afford to be more aggressive but do not trust the stock market. If you are one of them, you owe it to yourself and your family to be candid about this concern.

If both indicators point to an aggressive portfolio, then consider putting as much as 75% of your money in stock funds, balancing small-cap funds against large, and U.S. stock funds against foreign to dampen some of the volatility. The remaining 25% should be split between investment-grade bonds and cash. If your temperament or circumstances don't permit such an aggressive stance, a better fit might be 60% stocks, 20% bonds and 20% cash. Over the past 10 years, that would have provided 95% of the return earned by the aggressive portfolio with a loss in its worst year just 60% as large. And if your needs call for still more caution, try 50% stock funds, 20% bonds and 30% cash. This would have cut the worst-year loss to just 36% of the aggressive portfolio's and still have delivered 88% of the riskier brew's return.

Don't forget to stash enough cash. Before you risk any of your money, set aside an emergency reserve equal to three to six months' living expenses in a safe, easily accessible investment like a money fund. This will keep you from having to sell long-term investments if you become ill or lose your job. If the cash portion of your portfolio is large enough, it can serve as the emergency stash. If not, you'll need a separate reserve fund. In addition, if you're counting on income from your investments to meet day-to-day expenses, make sure that you allocate enough to bond or total return stock funds to meet your income needs before apportioning the rest of your portfolio.

Consider how many funds you can manage. When diversifying, don't confuse quantity with quality. What matters is not how many funds you own but how distinct they are. A portfolio of 10 small-cap growth funds is less truly diversified than one holding just a stock fund and a money-market fund. In general, you should aim for the broadest portfolio you can afford using the following guidelines based on the amount of capital that you have on hand for investment.

With $5,000 or less, go for a single diversified fund. You might consider balanced funds, which divide your money between stocks and bonds. For still more diversification, try asset allocation funds. They create a portfolio in a single fund, holding stocks, bonds and cash, and occasionally real estate, gold and overseas stocks.

With $5,000 to $20,000, you can afford three or four funds. If you started with a balanced fund and can tolerate moderate risk, you probably should think about adding a couple of stock funds with different approaches (e.g., a large-company growth fund and a small-cap fund). If you hate paperwork, you should consider sticking to funds in a single no-load family that will report all your investment transactions on one statement.

With $20,000 to $50,000, five or six funds ought to be enough. Depending on how you're allocating your assets to match your circumstances, you could add an overseas fund and an intermediate-term bond fund (one with maturities between five and 10 years). For less volatility and more income, think about going with two stock funds, two bond funds with intermediate maturities, and a money fund.

With $50,000 to $100,000, you can add another fund or two to further subdivide your stock and bond allocations. Among your stockholdings, you can balance growth against value funds; small-stock against large-company; domestic against foreign. Bond choices can be split among funds with varying maturities and levels of credit risk. Some investors also divide their stake in each subdivision between a couple of funds to balance one manager against the other.

With $100,000 or more, you have the wherewithal to hold 15 or 20 different funds. Note, however, that you would be adequately diversified with a well-chosen seven to 10. Owning more funds is fine if you have the time to track them. But if you break your holdings into many pieces smaller than $5,000, the diversification may not justify the record keeping. One way to streamline the office work is to buy no-load funds through the "no transaction fee" services of discount brokers like Charles Schwab and Fidelity Investments (see Chapter 5).

Move into the market methodically. Once you decide how to allocate the money in your portfolio, try to resist the urge to invest it all at once. Instead, divide the money into equal dollar amounts and move it into your chosen funds once a month or once a quarter over a year or two. Such periodic investing, commonly called dollar cost averaging, forces you to buy more fund shares when the prices are low and fewer when they are high—one of investing's golden rules explained in the next section. Another advantage of this technique is that it keeps you from yielding to panic in a market downturn.

 ## Four Techniques to Reduce Risk

Are you sitting on the sidelines because the stock market looks too scary? Or waiting for prices to hit bottom before moving more money into stock funds? Either way, you are very likely to be disappointed. No one really knows when stock prices have no place to go but up. As a result, you may miss the chance to make some big profits. Thus investing experts often suggest that you use a risk-reducing technique for moving money into stock funds that will let you take full advantage of price dips, prevent you from getting badly hurt by sudden spikes and help assure that you reach your financial goals. The strategy, called periodic investing, has you invest regularly (e.g., every month or quarter) no matter what's happening in the market. Here are four variations of this disciplined approach to investing.

Dollar cost averaging. With this most basic form of periodic investing, you put a set amount each month (say, $200) in a stock fund. When stock prices fall, your $200 buys more fund shares. When prices rise, your money buys fewer. That way, you keep your fund shares' average cost relatively low. As the table on the next page shows, if you had invested $200 a month from 1984 to 1993 in Vanguard Index Trust-500, which mimics the S&P 500 index, your $24,000 would have more than doubled to $49,400.

Dollar cost averaging is simple and very dependable. But you might prefer to boost your profits with a more advanced version, called progressive dollar cost averaging. This strategy takes into account inflation, the chief drawback of investing the same amount every month for years. With progressive averaging, you can increase your monthly contribution every year, or even every six months, by a set percentage. How much? Experts often

Profit from the Installment Plan

If you had used the value averaging method during the 1984 to 1993 bull market, you would have earned annual returns of 15%, far more than with any of the other risk-cutting strategies shown below and explained in this chapter. In today's increasingly skittish market, however, investing experts say the three other techniques may carry less risk. In our table, we assumed that a hypothetical investor had an account with the Vanguard Index Trust-500 Fund, which closely mimics the S&P 500 index. In the case of two related strategies, constant ratio planning and variable installment, we linked the Index Trust-500 with the Vanguard Money Market Reserves Prime Fund.

STRATEGY	Monthly contribution	Total amt. invested	Portfolio value	Average annual return	Avg. cost per share
Value averaging	Varies	$23,540	$49,400	15.1%	$20.90
Dollar cost averaging	$200	24,000	49,400	13.8	21.30
Constant ratio planning	200	24,000	40,400	9.9	28.00
Variable installment	200	24,000	40,300	9.9	29.30

recommend a manageable 10%. That will keep you far ahead of inflation as well as supercharge your savings. So an investor who starts out contributing $200 a month might step that up to $220 a year later. If you had used this technique from 1984 to 1993, your $37,950 total investment in the Vanguard Index Trust-500 would have grown to $69,800.

Value averaging. Think of this as dollar cost averaging with attitude. Rather than investing a set monthly amount, you put in whatever is necessary to hit your goal. Let's say you need $9,000 in three years for a down payment on a house. You first open a fund account with, perhaps, $200. Next, with the help of a financial calculator or compound interest tables found in your local library's reference section, you determine that your account's value must increase $200 a month to reach your target. The actual amount you invest each month will change as stock prices fluctuate. For example, if the market is flat during the month you open your fund account, you simply invest an additional $200 in the second month, bringing your account's value to $400. On the other hand, if your fund's value falls by 12.5% during the second month, your account will dip to $350. Your third investment must then be $250, since your game plan calls for your account to be worth $600 in month three. If, however, stocks rise in the second month and boost your balance to $470, your third contribution must be only $130.

What happens if the value of your holdings rises so rapidly that your account's value exceeds your monthly target? In that case, value averaging calls for you to sell some shares. If your account increased to $700 in the third month, you would dump $100 of your holdings. Of course, your profit would be taxable if you were investing outside of a tax-deferred account, such as an IRA. Therefore, you might prefer a modified value averaging strategy called no-sell value averaging. With this technique, when your portfolio value exceeds the target, you simply do nothing that month.

Value averaging beats dollar cost averaging roughly 90% of the time, calculates Michael Edleson, a Harvard Business School professor and author of the book *Value Averaging: The Safe and Easy Strategy for Higher Investment Returns*. In order to accumulate your $49,400 in Vanguard Index Trust-500, as shown in the table, you would have had to invest $24,000 from 1984 to 1993 if you used dollar cost averaging but $23,540 with value averaging. That $460 saving may seem slim. Still, your money would have worked more efficiently, delivering both higher returns and a lower average cost per share.

Constant ratio planning. This fairly conservative method calls for you to balance a stock fund investment against a less aggressive one, usually a money-market fund. You first decide how much risk you can take, then allocate your monthly investment between the two funds accordingly. Let's say you decide to split a $200 monthly investment evenly between a stock fund and a money fund. If stock prices rise, you eventually will have to shift money from your stock fund to your money fund to restore your fifty-fifty ratio. Investing experts recommend that you rebalance your portfolio whenever the ratio gets five percentage points out of whack (in our example, whenever the value of either fund rises to 55% of your portfolio). When stocks are rising, as they were from 1984 to 1993, the more risk you're willing to take when you set the ratio, the more money you will make. As the accompanying table shows, a $200 monthly investment divided equally between the Vanguard Index Trust-500 and the Vanguard Money Market Reserves Prime funds would have grown to $40,400, about $9,000 less than with straight dollar averaging. But you would cut your risk roughly in half by stashing 50% of your cash in a money fund.

Variable installment strategy. Like constant ratio, you start out by dividing your monthly investment equally between the funds. Then, when one fund lags the other, you direct your entire contribution to it. That way, you buy more shares when they are cheap and avoid putting money in investment categories that may be temporarily overvalued. Let's again assume you decide to invest $200 a month in a stock and a money fund. You start out by putting $100 into each. Whenever the stock fund's share price drops by an amount (say, 5%) that you have determined in advance, you put all of your next monthly investment into that fund. Conversely, if its share price rises 5%, you invest all your next monthly installment in the money fund. From 1984 to 1993, if you had invested a total of $24,000 using this 5% variable installment method, your portfolio would have grown to $40,300. Like constant ratio, variable installment would have earned you about $9,000 less than straight dollar cost averaging but would have carried much less risk.

Tend to Your IRA and Other Plans

The virtues of mutual funds make them ideally suited for self-directed Individual Retirement Accounts, Simplified Employee Pensions (SEPs) and Keogh plans. True, changes in federal tax law have reduced or eliminated some of the tax-sheltering benefits of an IRA. But many investors who bemoan their loss of the IRA deduction overlook the fact that the account's most important benefit remains—namely, long-term, tax-deferred compounding of their retirement funds. While you may no longer be eligible for the deduction, you still have the responsibility to manage your IRA and make it grow.

Let's start with the basics. An employed person may be entitled to fund an IRA with tax-deductible contributions of up to $2,000 per year ($2,250 a year for a couple with a nonworking spouse). You can fully deduct your contribution if you are not covered by a pension plan or if you earn less than $25,000 (single) or $40,000 (married and filing jointly). All earnings generated in the account accumulate tax-deferred until the funds are withdrawn. Early withdrawals (those made before age 59.5) are subject to a 10% tax penalty as well as ordinary income taxes.

When plotting your IRA strategy, with or without the deduction, you should follow the same general guidelines that you would for any fund investment. For example, an IRA that you plan to tap within five years should be invested conservatively in income or money funds, while cash that you won't need to touch for many years can be invested for growth in stock funds. If you have a substantial non-IRA portfolio of funds, however, you probably should avoid putting really aggressive growth funds in your retirement account. Why? In an IRA, the losses from a volatile fund can't be used to offset capital gains from others, as is the case with taxable profits realized on investments outside your IRA. Also keep in mind how an IRA fits into your overall retirement savings, including company-sponsored plans, and whether the funds you're considering help to diversify those assets.

♦ Two

Gunning for Long-Term Growth

I magine that you are about to mail a check to your money-market fund when a genie suddenly appears and makes you the following offer. "Give the check to me instead for at least five years, and I'll make it grow much faster than your money fund could. If you need your money back sooner, however, you may not get it all." While the genie's challenge may sound fantastical, it's one that you face every time you invest for growth in stock funds. History shows that the stock market returns about 2.7 times as much as do money-market funds and twice as much as bonds in the long term. But from one month or one year to the next you can lose serious money, as anyone who owned a stock fund in October 1987 can tell you. In that crash-marred month, stock funds plunged an average of 22%.

The fear of losing so much dough is understandable. But it is the wrong worry if you are five or more years away from your financial goals. When you're investing for the long term, your biggest risk is inflation, not a sudden selling panic on Wall Street. And only the stock market has delivered high enough returns over time to keep you advancing against the head wind of rising prices. For example, Bob and Kris Mahre of Lakeville, Minn. recognized the need for such returns soon after they married (see "Scrupulous Savers Agree to Get Aggressive" on the page opposite). The couple started by putting $1,000 away in their first pick, overseas stock fund Scudder International. They've since added other stock funds and faithfully contribute $300 a month to them. "We're picking the most aggressive funds we can find," says Bob, "because we're young enough to ride out the dips in the market."

Steeling yourself for market risk is only the first challenge of betting on stock funds. The second is choosing the right funds. Simply being invested is no guarantee of strong returns. In 1993, a vintage year for stock funds, their returns averaged some 12%. But shareholders of the Frontier Equity growth fund lost 25%, while those in Govett Smaller Companies made 59%. Now no amount of analysis can help you identify next year's No. 1 fund (that power is beyond even genies). But by grasping the most important elements of a fund manager's investment style, you can understand why a fund is a leader or laggard and how it is likely to behave in the future.

The possibility of short-term losses is a constant in today's increasingly edgy market. So a prudent investor will take some elementary precautions. For starters, don't consider investing in stock funds unless you're reasonably sure you won't need the money within five years (roughly the length of the typical economic cycle). If you were unlucky enough to put your money in at a market peak, you may need the full cycle to recover your losses and make a profit. If you suffer a 30% loss in your first year of investing, for example, it would take you almost four years at a 10% annual return to get even. The best way to avoid such unfortunate timing is to ease into your funds gradually by making equal payments over a matter of months or years, regardless of whether the stock market is rising or falling (see "Four Techniques to Reduce Risk" in the previous chapter).

Scrupulous Savers Agree to Get Aggressive

Bob and Kris Mahre of Lakeville, Minn. came to an unsettling realization just six months after their wedding. "We had two good incomes yet couldn't figure out where all our money was going," recalls Bob, 32, a sales engineer for W.L. Gore & Associates, the maker of Teflon and Gore-Tex. Admits Kris, 30, a reservations sales agent for Northwest Airlines: "We didn't have the best habits." So the couple hired a local fee-only financial planner who convinced them to invest $300 a month in a thriving portfolio of no-load funds. "It's wonderful to get these monthly statements showing how much our savings are growing," says Kris. Chimes in Bob: "We both work too hard not to pay ourselves first."

Aiming for distant goals. The Mahres are saving primarily for their infant son Adam's college education and their own retirement. Thus their horizons are long term, and they're focusing on growth-oriented stock funds. "History shows that stocks outperform any other investment over time," says Bob. Every month the Mahres invest $100 in each of three stock funds using a technique called dollar cost averaging that is explained in detail in the previous chapter. When picking the funds, Bob screened for those with five-year annual returns in the low to mid-teens. "I want steady funds we can stick with for a long time," he says. "I avoid those earning 25% to 30%. There's no way returns that high can last."

Assembling a broad portfolio. He chose the Nicholas Fund for its concentration on small and medium-size companies. To bring dimension to the portfolio, he bought Twentieth Century Select Investors, which favors established growth stocks like Wal-Mart. He admits that another purchase, Scudder International, has had disappointing recent returns. But he and Kris aren't giving up on it. The Mahres also own Vanguard Wellington, a balanced portfolio of stocks and bonds, and don't worry they're too heavily invested in stocks. "I'd feel uneasy," says Bob, "if we owned individual stocks. By choosing different types of stock funds, we're diversified in a diversified product." To ensure that they remain on course, they meet quarterly with their financial planner.

Itching to invest more. Bob says that he would love to be sinking $600 or more a month into stock funds but concedes that Kris, who handles the family's day-to-day finances, is a more conservative investor. "Bob gets excited and wants to plunge ahead," she says good-naturedly. "But I like to take things more slowly." Bob buys that. "With time and mutual funds on our side," he figures, "I don't think we can go wrong."

Reach for Double-Digit Returns

More and more investors whose goal is growth are focusing on fund managers' investment styles for the simple reason that people differ on what makes a stock appealing. By training or temperament, managers gravitate toward stocks with certain traits. Some favor those of small companies (market values under $500 million). Others like large blue-chip firms (over $2 billion). And still others prefer companies in the middle called mid-caps. Within those sizes, managers may seek either fast-growing firms or seeming bargains. Learning where your fund fits in is more than just pigeonholing. Academic studies show that style accounts for at least 75% of a typical growth fund's return.

Small vs. large companies. Each of these two approaches has its own investment logic and its own roster of successful practitioners. Small-cap or mid-cap managers such as John Laporte of T. Rowe Price New Horizons and T. Rowe Price New America Growth, for instance, specialize in the stocks of small and medium-size companies on the theory that young, entrepreneurial firms have the most explosive growth potential. The risk, however, is that small-stock funds are prone to unpredictable downturns that can swiftly wipe out 10% to 20% of their value. In contrast, a manager such as Michael Gordon of Fidelity Blue Chip Growth prefers the stocks of corporate giants. The argument for them is that they are Wall Street's best source of stable profits. The problem is that it's hard for even the shrewdest managers to uncover hidden opportunities among the most widely followed stocks.

Growth vs. value approach. After size, the main style distinction is between so-called growth and value investors. The former want to own the fastest growing, most successful companies (e.g., the Microsofts, Wal-

Marts, Home Depots and their successors) capable of expanding their earnings a brisk 15% or better a year. The problem is that such premium companies usually trade at rich prices relative to their earnings. Thus their stocks can fall hard in the event that earnings fail to live up to investors' lofty expectations. Value managers such as Kent Simons and Larry Marx of Neuberger & Berman Guardian are the stock market's equivalent of flea market browsers. They're looking for cast-aside stocks trading at prices that may not reflect the true value of their assets or future earnings. "We are looking for strong companies where we think bad news has knocked the price down unfairly," says Simons. And a few managers straddle the growth and value divide, including such standouts as Mark Tincher and David Klassen of Vista Capital Growth.

How do you discern a manager's style? For size distinctions, simply call the fund sponsor and ask for the fund's median market capitalization, or the total market value of the fund's median stock. To tell whether the manager is a growth getter or value seeker, look at the fund's yield and price-earnings ratio (calculated by references like Morningstar). A value fund generally will have a higher than average yield and a lower than average PE ratio. A growth fund will be the opposite.

Which size or style is best? Research suggests that over the long haul, small-company stocks beat out big ones, and value stocks have the edge over growth. For example, Trinity Investment Management based in Cambridge, Mass. studied growth vs. value stocks over a recent 24-year stretch and found that value won, returning 12% annually relative to growth's 9%. Here's one rationale. Because value stocks by definition already trade at depressed prices, they tend to fall less far in bear markets. In the five losing markets included in the Trinity study, value stocks dropped an average of about 17%, while the typical growth stock lost 25%. As for small-caps, Trinity's calculations show that these stocks edged out large companies by nearly one percentage point a year (or 10.4% to 9.6%). Over shorter time spans, however, it's a much tighter race in which each of the different styles takes its turn in the lead for periods that generally last two to five years.

Trying to predict precisely when the cycle is going to shift is as futile as any other kind of market timing. That's why choosing among investment styles is primarily a tool of diversification. By owning some stock funds of every style, you can effectively smooth out the inevitable ups and downs of Wall Street fashions. Just as important, you'll be able to distinguish between fund managers who are lagging merely because their investment approach is out of vogue and those who simply have lost their touch.

That said, you can still use your knowledge of styles to angle for extra return at the margin by tilting your portfolio toward the favored group. For example, over the past three years, small and mid-cap stocks have generally outperformed the big fellas. Most analysts believe this trend will continue, with some arguing that mid-caps could be the chief beneficiaries. They note that it is easier for large institutions to take positions in mid-caps than in truly small stocks. Thus as pension funds and other institutions increasingly switch from large stocks to smaller ones, mid-caps could provide investors with the biggest kick. By the same token, many analysts expect value stocks to keep beating growth companies. Reason: value funds tend to invest heavily in cyclical industries, such as steel and paper, that profit the most from a strong economic upturn such as the current one.

Picking the right fund for you. Once you've identified the investment style that you want to add to your portfolio, your next job is to find a fund that executes it with aplomb. Style may account for about three-quarters of a typical stock fund's long-term performance. But this statistical edge still leaves 25% or more that can be explained only by the manager's skill.

Start your search by looking for consistency. A record of strong past performance is more likely to be sustained if it was built on sturdy returns year after year rather than erratic flashes of brilliance. "No. 1 funds rarely repeat," says Christopher Poll of the Boston fund ranking service Micropal Inc. "But a fund that consistently ranks in the top half of its category will have superior long-term returns." Then make sure that your fund doesn't dish out more pain during market downturns than you can take. Check the fund's return during falling markets. Could you sit through a 33% swan dive, for example, such as John Hancock Special Equities took during the last bear market? If not, you might prefer a fund like Aim Charter. It lately has achieved a less Olympian five-year gain than the Hancock fund but absorbed a more bearable loss in the last market slump.

Also check assets under management. As fund popularity booms, funds that come into the public eye can quickly balloon by hundreds of millions of dollars. For example, after briefly winding up atop the growth fund performance charts, the once obscure Monetta Fund rapidly swelled from $150 million to more than $450 million. That kind of cash flow can be particularly hard on small-company funds, some of whose holdings may have only $50,000 worth of shares change hands daily. As a rule, you should think twice about hanging on to small-cap funds with assets of more than $500 million.

Shareholders in blue-chip stock funds usually don't have to worry about asset size. That's some consolation for holding funds in a style that has been on a slower track. Of course, big-cap stocks still have a role in your portfolio as a more stable counterpoint to riskier small-stock funds. And as the rise and fall of investment styles over time has shown, one thing you can be sure of is that one day blue chips will grab the lead—again.

Broaden Your Profits Overseas

Before you ship some of your fund portfolio offshore, keep in mind that U.S. stocks, not foreign ones, have been the world champs over a recent five-year period. The score: the S&P 500 index returned 9% annually vs.

just 3% for Morgan Stanley's EAFE index representing the major stock markets outside the U.S. Over the next five years, however, overseas markets seem destined to out-perform. One reason, argues Peter Lynch, ex-skipper of Fidelity Magellan, is that "stocks outside the U.S. tend to be not as well covered and more undervalued." Today's booming foreign markets also reflect mounting optimism that the global slump in industrial countries will soon be history, unleashing more capital investment in rapidly modernizing regions like Asia and Latin America. Thus developing economies should continue to be the most exciting destinations for investors, given those countries' projected growth of 4% to 8% a year, vs. the 2.5% to 3% recoveries hoped for in Europe, Japan and the U.S.

Where to begin? Overseas funds are ideal if you lack the resolve to become fluent in faraway markets. There are four subcategories based upon breadth of investing focus. The broadest are global funds, which can invest anywhere in the world including the U.S., followed by international funds, which invest everywhere in the world except the U.S. Then there are regional funds, which invest in a specific segment of the globe such as Latin America, and single-country funds.

The case for going international. Investors first beginning to diversify worldwide can probably cut through the confusion of choices by ignoring global and single-country funds and zeroing in on internationals. Why? The problem with global funds is that the manager's freedom to acquire U.S. stocks can negate your whole purpose of buying the fund—to diversify over-seas. The typical global fund today puts some 40% of its assets in the U.S. Thus if you're aiming to reallocate a portfolio mix to contain, say, one-quarter holdings abroad, you could calibrate that percentage more pre-cisely with an international fund, a pure overseas play. And many small investors will find single-country funds too risky, narrowly focused or both.

You have already read how spreading your domestic investments over a variety of industries and companies that perform well under varying conditions reduces your risk in seesawing market cycles. So it stands to reason that branching out into foreign stocks further diminishes your downside when the U.S. market takes one of its periodic tumbles. The investment management firm Bingham Osborn & Scarborough in San Francisco provides an example of two hypothetical investors over the past 20 years. One had 80% of her assets in U.S. stocks and 20% in foreign markets; the other had all of his assets in U.S. stocks. She was smarter than he. While the internationally diversified investor faced 6% lower overall risk as measured by price swings, her returns were slightly higher (both she and the all-American investor gained close to 13% annually over the period).

Weigh the political and currency risks. For many small investors, funds are often the only viable vehicles for venturing into uncharted international waters. Most foreign stock markets do not impose reporting standards on companies that are as stringent as those enforced by the Securities and Exchange Commission here. So such financial information is not only harder to obtain but also tends to be less reliable. Worse, buying foreign securities exposes you to two special types of risk. The first is political risk, or the danger that unexpected electoral shifts or governmental instability will adversely affect a market. For example, shares in the closed-end Mexico Fund tumbled following the assassination of the leading presidential candidate. The other worry that's commonly looming over foreign investing is currency risk, the danger that the lately anemic value of the U.S. dollar abroad will rebound and shrink your returns overseas.

Suppose, for example, you take $1,000 and convert it into Japanese yen at a time when the dollar is worth 100 yen. Then you spend those 100,000 yen on 100 shares of a Japanese stock at 1,000 yen per share. What would happen if the dollar rises in value to 125 yen but your stock goes nowhere? If you decided to bail out, you would get the same price you paid (100,000 yen) but net only $800 after converting your proceeds back into dollars (100,000 divided by 125). So you lost 20% (not counting brokerage commissions) on your investment even though your stock held firm. Of course, if the dollar fell the same percent against the yen, you would have profited 20% on that stagnant stock. The reassuring news is that currency swings tend to cancel each other out over the long term, leaving no significant statistical impact on portfolio performance. But the short-term currency threat may rule out the notion of international diversification for some conservative investors.

Keep It Simple with Indexers

Finding funds that beat the market averages would seem to be the natural goal of every investor. But beginning in 1983, the stock fund average got whupped for eight straight years by the S&P 500 index. Slowly it began to dawn on people that settling for a low-expense fund that just tried to match the index was the better part of valor. Following the lockstep lead of giant pension funds, individuals started to switch into indexing and a strategy was born. After all, says the top proponent and marketer of index funds, Vanguard Group chairman John Bogle: "There are a lot stupider ways to invest."

Today there are scores of entries that describe themselves as index funds. Looking for a fund to match the S&P 500? Or the S&P Mid-Cap 400? Or the Wilshire 4500? No problem. Nowadays, Vanguard and its many competitors offer index funds to track almost every imaginable slice of the securities markets, including those overseas, plus a new group of superindexers that are called quant funds (see "These Funds Look for a Quant Leap" on page 46). Some forecasters predict that within 20 years index funds could jump from their recent 3% share of stock fund total assets to as much as 30%.

It's possible that this proliferation could become too much of a relatively good thing. True, there are stupider ways to invest. But there are smarter ones too within certain fund groups. Indexing is most competitive in the

S&P 500 stocks and in high-grade bonds where the performance differentials between the leading and the laggard funds are smallest. Skip the indexers in categories where you have a better shot at outgaining them, including small-company, value and international funds. In these the stock-picking superstars among managers (and fund players who invest with them) can frequently outshine both the market indexes and the middling funds.

When indexing makes sense. These funds tend to shine in the largest, most liquid financial markets followed by the most pros. The S&P 500 stocks and quality bonds, to cite two examples, trade in so-called efficient markets (those in which legions of analysts scrutinize the companies and pass along to investors information and predictions about earnings or credit quality). It's difficult in such markets for fund managers to steal a big march on their peers. The main difference in returns, particularly among bond funds, often boils down to the drag of advisory fees, brokerage commissions and other expenses. Thus the best index funds have an edge because they're spared the cost of well-paid managerial talent and require minimal trading. Indeed, the S&P 500 index funds with the lowest expenses have periodically outperformed managed stock funds in their category. At the same time, those few index funds that have the gall to impose high expenses for this no-brainer bracket tend to lag behind their competitors.

Before examining the pros and cons of index funds category by category, you should note that even the Vanguard Group's apostles of indexing don't themselves totally practice what they promote in their personal portfolios. An analysis of documents filed with the SEC indicates that less than 30% of chairman Bogle's holdings in Vanguard stock funds are index funds, with the rest in actively managed Vanguard portfolios. Vanguard president John Brennan, heir apparent to Bogle, has an even lower 10% in index funds. A Vanguard spokesperson explained that, as fund directors, both Brennan and Bogle have a responsibility to own a wide array of

These Funds Look for a Quant Leap

Games-loving computer nuts who trade securities with quantitative techniques, better known as quants, first became part of the public parlance in *Liar's Poker*, the rollicking tell-all book about Wall Street powerhouse Salomon Bros. Now these quant types have brought their computer mojo to mutual fund land, merrily hacking away in hopes of outperforming the major market indexes. Although it is probably premature to judge for sure, their preliminary results are promising.

Pedal to the metal. Quant fund managers drive down the same road as indexers but with an extra flourish. Quants cut corners, jettison baggage they regard as unnecessary and push the speed limit. The typical quant fund relies only on quantifiable numbers, not subjective judgments about a company, and starts out targeting a particular index. Then the manager tweaks the portfolio mix toward those industries, specific stocks or bond maturities that the printouts indicate will beat the benchmark. Although most quant funds key in on the S&P 500 index, their computerized information scanning can also score in less efficient markets, such as small-company stocks, ignored by many analysts.

Leader of the quant pack. That distinction currently belongs to Brad Lewis, an Annapolis-trained, ex-Navy chopper pilot. Over a recent five-year period, his Fidelity Disciplined Equity returned 13% annually, vs. 9% for the S&P 500. Lewis' software is a form of so-called artificial intelligence (employing what are known as neural networks). The system seeks to go beyond the usual investing screens to reveal obscure patterns in financial data such as earnings growth, book value, dividend payout ratios and debt levels that seem associated with higher stock returns. The patterns are then remembered and applied in future screens. Fidelity Disciplined Equity does stick close to the industry weightings in the S&P 500. If oil stocks represent 10% of the index, Lewis will keep his portfolio between 8.5% and 11.5% in oils. His performance edge comes from using his computer to pick the best oils, which often are smaller and more entrepreneurial companies than those in the index.

Fixed-income superindexers. Quants came to bond funds in 1990 when Mary Ellen Stanek began running the Portico Bond Immdex Fund, which aims to match the Lehman Bros. composite bond index. Her fund strives to quant its way to an additional 0.5% return each year. Says Stanek: "We hope to deliver the index return even after our portfolio's 0.5% expenses are deducted." A noble aim that only time can test.

           Gunning for Long-Term Growth

funds. In addition, Vanguard says the chairman's asset allocation owes in part to a large build-up of shares in Vanguard's Windsor Fund, which Bogle has held and reinvested since its founding in 1958. For the rest of us, there are other arguments why indexing is not the panacea that takes all the effort out of fund picking.

When indexing doesn't make sense. The lead in the stock market seesaws back and forth over the years between large and small companies. So long as the behemoths stayed in front, as was the case for the five years to 1991, the typical stock fund suffered from a congenital disadvantage. That's because its portfolio concentrated on small and mid-cap stocks with a weighted median market value of $5 billion, vs. about $13 billion for the S&P 500. Since November 1990, however, small and mid-cap stocks have outgained the big ones. The shift in the market became apparent by 1991, when stock funds as a group outperformed the S&P 500 index by 37% to 31%. This could be the start of a repeat of the 1977-82 pattern, when small stocks trounced large ones, 264% to 63%. In that six-year span, stock funds slaughtered the S&P 500 by 146% to 78%. Says John Laporte, manager of the small-cap T. Rowe Price New Horizons Fund: "I figure small-company shares will outgain big stocks by as many as 10 percentage points annually for another couple of years."

Indexing also underperforms in markets where strong research pays off. As the size of companies declines, so does the number of Wall Street analysts who track them. As a general rule, the smaller the company, the better the odds that an alert fund manager can uncover its glittering prospects ahead of the herd, buy its stock cheaply and then reap a bundle by the time the rest of the Street gets in on the secret. This rule helps explains why small stock funds as a group have outpaced the Vanguard Small Capitalization Stock index fund over both the past three and five years. And there are additional complications for investors seeking the seeming simplicity and diversity of a small-cap index fund. To start with, there is no one clear benchmark comparable to large stocks' S&P 500. Competing small-cap measures include the Russell 2000 and the Wilshire 4500. As the titles of these indexes suggest, they include a lot of obscure stocks that may be relatively illiquid.

In such thinly traded stocks, the heavy-footed moves of the indexers can compound the already scary volatility. (In fact, most small stock index funds do not buy every single stock but use a statistical technique known as tracking to approximate the price movement of many stocks without actually owning them.) Another problem is that indexers buy a lot of dogs and cats along with good companies. Yet focusing on just the few good companies is precisely what the top small-company managers do best. Expert research to ferret out the best stocks also distinguishes the champion overseas funds.

The latest wrinkle, value vs. growth. If indexing performs better in the largest tier of the market, how does the technique work in that corner of it where so-called value investors hang out? Big stocks dominate here, of course. So it must follow that indexing pays off for fundholders seeking to hitch their fortunes to value stocks. Not so fast. As with small stocks, the value approach depends on intensive research to recognize when an unfashionable company has a stronger outlook than the rest of Wall Street realizes. When big-name stocks are knocked down by bad news, sharp-penciled value managers can often identify the ones that figure to rebound fastest and highest.

Still, if you want a low-cost vehicle for betting on value investing or its rival growth approach, you can find both at (who else?) Vanguard. It has two index funds that divide the S&P 500 stocks into value and growth segments. Vanguard Index Trust: Value Portfolio has a below-average ratio of price to book value and above-average dividend yields. Vanguard Index Trust: Growth Portfolio specializes in shares that have the highest price-book ratios and lower dividend growth. There is another spin on indexing that aims at reducing risk. Gateway Index Plus Fund hedges by selling call options and, when its manager senses danger, purchasing put options on the S&P 100-stock index (the biggest stocks measured by total market value). Over the past five years, Gateway's return has kept pace with stock funds as a group while exposing investors to a risk level a fifth that of the norm.

 ## Speculate with Specialty Funds

Index funds are great for invest-and-forget shareholders. But what if you get a kick from actively speculating with a portion of your shareholdings—your mad money, so to speak—in hopes of making a quick killing? Or want to own some gold to hedge your bond funds against the risk that inflation will unexpectedly come roaring back? In such cases, the most sensible way to place your bets is through specialty stock funds, often called sector funds because they tend to concentrate their holdings in a single industry, such as natural resources, or service area like health care or asset class such as gold and real estate.

Of course, a fund invested in today's hottest sector will outperform almost all diversified stock funds. One reason is that diversified funds will contain stocks in weak as well as strong fields. With these inherently volatile funds, as with individual stocks, you decide which industry group is likely to be most profitable. The difference is that with a specialty fund you rely on a manager to assemble and monitor a portfolio of the most promising stocks within that group. The challenge is to pick the industries that are poised to become market leaders and to avoid the pacesetters that are about to stumble—specialty funds usually dominate short-term rankings of both the best and worst performers.

The odds are not in your favor. With all its eggs in one basket, a specialty fund can fall much faster than diversified ones when market sentiment turns against its industry. Compounding the risk is the fact that investors can't rely on sector fund performance records in the same way as with other funds. With conventional funds, a superior record reflects a manager's decisions about when to buy and sell stocks in different industries. With sector funds, recent strong performance by the industry doesn't mean the trend will continue. Indeed, the hotter the fund, the more likely the industry could hit a down cycle soon. Yet sector fund managers typically must stay mostly invested in the designated industry; they usually can switch no more than 20% of assets into cash or bonds as defensive measures.

Even continuing good news about an industry's prospects can create problems for specialty fund managers and prospective shareholders. As investors' money pours into top-performing sector funds, their managers must chase a limited number of stocks, paying ever more as they climb. Then, often as the sector trend levels off after the initial spurt, the funds' sizzling recent returns keep precipitating a torrent of new shareholder money. The late arrivals, however, get nothing like the soaring results that inspired their investment. That's because the fund managers can't find enough promising places to invest the new cash.

Mindful of the peril, you can profit from specialty funds in two ways. One is to buy them as turbocharged aggressive growth funds, riding out the fluctuations in share value in hopes of hefty profits down the line. If you choose an industry with seemingly strong long-term prospects, you could do better over time than you would with a diversified growth fund. As with any highly volatile fund, however, you should invest only cash that you don't expect to need for at least five years. A more common use is as flat-out speculations. With this approach you try to buy into a fund just as its sector hits bottom and sell when it reaches a peak—a nifty feat even among the most successful professional traders. The technique is best used by experienced investors as a less hazardous way to speculate in individual stocks. That is, you could correctly identify the next hot industry but still pick the stocks that fizzle early. Funds avoid that pitfall by holding dozens of issues.

✦ Three

Aiming for Reliable Income

Income investors were taught some painful lessons by 1994's bond market sell-off, which was triggered largely by Federal Reserve hikes in interest rates. Foremost among them is that maturity still matters. Long-term U.S. Treasury bonds (those maturing in more than 10 years) fell 8% in a four-month period, compared with just 3% for government bonds of short and intermediate terms (one to 10 years). The decline showed the risks of two income-boosting gimmicks, leverage and derivatives. Leverage, or borrowing to buy additional bonds, juices returns when interest rates are flat or falling. But it magnifies losses when rates rise. Derivatives are investment concoctions like options that amount in their most common form to little more than bets on the direction of interest rates. Fund managers whose derivatives helped plump up income as rates dropped over the early 1990s were suddenly hit with 9% to 16% losses when rates headed up.

Despite such worrisome trends, income investors can still find solid funds that pay regular, generous dividends.

That's the reason why such funds are so attractive to retirees and other people who depend on investment earnings for a large portion of their everyday living expenses. Many growth-oriented investors also own income funds to help diversify their holdings and lower the risk inherent in fairly aggressive stock portfolios.

Why income funds are so popular. Most own lots of bonds, which obligate the issuing company or government to pay interest, usually at regular intervals, and to repay the face value of the bond at maturity. Some funds seek capital gains as a secondary goal by supplementing their bond holdings with high-dividend stocks or convertible securities. Convertibles are essentially hybrids (issued either as bonds or preferred stock) that pay fixed income the same way that bonds do but can be exchanged for shares of the issuing company's common stock at a specified price. A large number of funds also provide tax-exempt income by investing exclusively in municipal bonds issued by city and state governments.

The most closely watched yardstick of an income fund's performance is yield (the fund's annual dividend divided by the current price of its shares). When comparing yields, you should keep in mind that funds with nearly identical objectives do not necessarily calculate their yields in a uniform manner. Different funds measure earnings over different periods, and some try to fatten their dividends with income from options they sell on the bonds in their portfolios. Prodded by the SEC, funds have adopted standard methods of computing yields. But there's still lots of wiggle room (see "Cut Through the Yield Flimflam" on the next page).

Why total return is paramount. Remember that unlike a bank certificate of deposit, an income fund's payout isn't guaranteed. Your total return from a fund depends not only on the dividends you get but also on the price you receive when you sell your shares. The value of bonds (and the funds that own them) appreciates when interest rates decline and falls when interest

Cut Through the Yield Flimflam

As this chapter explains in detail, you can't judge a bond fund solely by its yield. Doing so ignores potential declines in a fund's share price. But there's another problem with yield figures. Sometimes they lie. The culprit: there are many defensible ways to calculate yield. Thus it's tempting for funds to quote whatever figure sounds highest even if it's misleading. Worse, some funds buy securities that temporarily inflate their yield at the expense of long-term returns.

The appeal of the 30-day yield. To get the most reliable picture of a bond fund's income potential, you should first consult its SEC yield, which is sometimes referred to as the 30-day yield. It's the only yield figure that regulators allow funds to cite in their ads or the recorded updates on their telephone lines. Note, however, that a fund family's phone reps may quote any figure they want. Funds calculate the 30-day yield according to a fairly strict, standardized SEC formula that projects the fund's past 30-day payout into the future and washes out any fancy yield-enhancing accounting.

The problem with the 12-month yield. You should also ask for the 12-month distribution rate, sometimes called the 12-month average yield. In contrast to the more hypothetical SEC number, the distribution rate tells you what the fund actually paid out over the previous year as a percentage of its current NAV (net asset value adjusted for any capital-gains distributions). But be careful here. This figure can be manipulated much more easily than the SEC yield. For example, funds can inflate their distribution rate by buying so-called premium bonds (high-yield issues that are selling for above their face value). The bond's higher payouts are offset by the fact that the bond's price is destined to fall as it approaches maturity. This unsettling fact, of course, isn't reflected in the distribution rate. The bonds in some U.S. Government funds, for example, might trade at 11% over their face value. And the distribution rate is one percentage point higher than that of comparable government bond funds. But the funds' NAV has shrunk 10% to 12% since 1986.

How to compare the two yields. If the distribution rate is more than one percentage point higher than the more strictly calculated SEC yield, it's a sign that the fund could be pumping up its yield artificially. When you find that sort of discrepancy, you should be aware that those enticing yield figures may be coming at the expense of your total return, which is the number that matters most to holders of bond funds.

rates increase. Generally speaking, the higher an income fund's yield, the greater the overall credit risk, maturity and volatility of the bonds the fund holds.

There is no credit risk, or likelihood of a bond's issuer defaulting on its interest or principal payments, among funds that invest solely in bonds or mortgage-backed securities guaranteed by the federal government. Nor should there be any fears over the safety of funds whose bond holdings have the highest credit ratings from Standard & Poor's or Moody's, which grade companies and municipalities from AAA (tops) to D (in default). Financially solid issuers pay the least to borrow money, so you get lower yields. To grab higher income, however, some funds concentrate on lower quality issues, commonly called junk bonds, that are rated less than investment grade (B or below). While remarkably few junk bonds have defaulted over time, they are the ones investors dump first when business conditions sour or bond prices slump across the board, causing their prices to drop the most.

Moreover, long-term bonds almost always yield more than short-term ones (maturing in five years or less) or intermediate issues (five to 10 years) because their prices are the most sensitive to fluctuations in interest rates. If rates were to rise by just one percentage point, the price of recently issued 20-year Treasury bonds would fall about 9%. Three-year Treasury notes would drop only 2% to 3%. So if you think interest rates are going to rise, as they did for much of the past year, consider funds that limit their holdings to bonds of short or intermediate terms. If you expect rates to fall, favor long-term bond funds. Each fund generally keeps its holdings' maturities within a range specified in the prospectus. To find out a fund's average maturity, you must call the fund.

 ## Your Best Buys in Bond Funds

Once you fully understand the risks, bond funds are a great way to pull in reliable income. They aren't just for income seekers, however. Another key role is to reduce the volatility of your portfolio. "Bonds make it possible to tolerate the risks of stocks," explains Roger Gibson, a Pittsburgh investment adviser. "When stocks plunge, bonds tend to fall less." Sometimes bonds even appreciate. According to the Chicago research firm Ibbotson Associates, in 15 of the past 20 years when stocks lost money, long-term bonds gained 6% on average.

Before you start picking funds, be advised they aren't always the most economical way to put bonds into your portfolio. If the only bonds you plan to buy are U.S. government issues, you may be better off getting yours directly from Uncle Sam (see "Buying U.S. Treasuries from the Source" on page 56). If you decide bond funds are your best fixed-income choice, avoid the mistake of assuming that today's entries are the sleepy little numbers your parents prized. Like every other kind of fund, bond funds require you to make sophisticated trade-offs between risk and reward. So you need to understand not only how bond funds work, and what they can do for you, but also what can go wrong.

Face up to interest-rate risk. The first thing many investors mistakenly look for in a bond fund is a high current yield. For one thing, the fat payouts that some aggressively managed funds have bragged about lately could owe more to accounting sleight-of-hand than investment brilliance. Besides, high yields give you little advantage over bank CDs if the value of your shares skids 5% to 6% in response to a spurt in rates.

Interest-rate risk is based on a sort of Newtonian Law of the bond market. When rates rise, prices of bonds fall. That's because potential buyers of previously issued bonds demand price cuts to compensate them for the old bonds' lower yields. Of course, the process also works in reverse. When rates fall, previously issued bonds become more valuable and their prices rise because they're now the ones with the comparatively loftier yields. As a rule, a bond's sensitivity to interest-rate moves decreases as it approaches maturity. That explains why short-term bond funds like T. Rowe Price Short-Term Bond (with maturi-

Buying U.S. Treasuries from the Source

It often makes more sense to buy Treasury securities directly rather than through a fund. Since there's no credit risk, you don't need a fund's diversification. And since the investments are, quite literally, commodities, you don't need a pro to select them. As Fidelity Magellan's former maestro Peter Lynch quips: "There's no point paying Yo Yo Ma to play a radio." You can buy Treasury bonds and notes without sales charges directly from the Federal Reserve. For an application, write the U.S. Treasury, Bureau of the Public Debt, Washington, D.C. 20239 or call the Bureau at 202-874-4000, ext. 232.

If you plan to reinvest your interest, however, Treasuries can be a hassle. For example, these days $10,000 worth of three-year notes generates just $218 every six months—too little to reinvest in more notes. One solution is to go with zero-coupon Treasuries, which make no regular interest payments. You buy zeros for a price that ranges from 10% to 90% of their face value, depending on the bonds' maturity. Your return is the difference between your purchase price and the face value, paid at maturity. Zeros are especially useful if you want to put your hands on a specific amount at a point in the future. For example, if you expect to need $20,000 for your 14-year-old's first year of college bills, you could invest $15,450 today for $20,000 worth of zeros maturing in four years. You buy zeros from a broker. Note, however, that you can minimize transaction costs, and avoid worry over the zeros' inherent volatility, by holding the securities to maturity.

ties recently averaging some 2.4 years) have as little as 20% of the volatility of long-term rivals like Vanguard Fixed Income: Long-Term U.S. Treasury (lately averaging around 22 years). Interest-rate risk helps explain another oddity of bond funds' performance. Most of them are strongest when the economy is weak. That's because economic slowdowns typically reduce loan demand and dampen inflation. Both factors tend to push interest rates down and, hence, drive bond prices higher.

Decide how much to sock into bonds. Many
advisers suggest that you build your bond fund portfolio around a conservative core of short/intermediate-term

taxable funds. The rationale: five-year Treasuries, for example, have yielded 93% as much as a 30-year Treasury with less than 50% of the interest-rate risk. As your bond portfolio grows, you can add funds of different maturities or credit quality, depending on your outlook for interest rates and tolerance of risk. But don't go fund crazy. Says Philadelphia financial planner Neil Kauffman: "You can diversify properly with just two or three funds." Here's a rundown of your fund choices.

U.S. Governments.
These funds invest in bonds issued by the U.S. Treasury or federal government agencies. The safety from default is all but absolute, which makes government funds tops for conservative income seekers. The trade-off is lower yields. Vanguard Fixed-Income: Long-Term U.S. Treasury, for example, recently paid slightly less than Vanguard Fixed-Income: Long-Term Corporate, a corporate fund of the same average maturity. Note, however, that in Treasury-only bond funds, the lower yield is at least partly made up by the fact that the dividends usually escape state taxes. Be aware too that government backing does not protect you against interest-rate risk. A Treasury portfolio will drop in price when interest rates rise.

Mortgage-backed securities.
One species of government fund specializes in these issues, which represent shares in investment pools consisting of home mortgages. They're backed by federal agencies with such cute nicknames as Ginnie Mae (the Government National Mortgage Association) and Freddie Mac (the Federal Home Loan Mortgage Corporation). They offer yields 0.5 to 1.5 percentage points higher than those on Treasury funds. The higher yields are partly a trade-off for prepayment risk, one peculiar to mortgage-backed securities. When interest rates fall, homeowners rush to refinance their mortgages at lower rates. As the old pooled mortgages are paid off, funds holding the securities are, in effect, handed back parts of their principal, which they then must reinvest at lower prevailing yields.

Thus mortgage funds get a far smaller boost than Treasuries from falling rates.

Corporates. Such bond funds allow you to invest in businesses ranging from America's most solid to its shakiest. Entries in our high-grade corporate category hold bonds carrying an average credit rating only a step below governments, making them an appealing alternative for investors who want to earn more than government funds pay but who don't want to get swamped by credit risk. At the other end of the credit spectrum are high-yield corporates, better known as junk bond funds. They focus on the bonds of debt-burdened behemoths and unproven start-ups. Unlike other bond funds, junkers are at their best in a strengthening economy because a healthy business climate reduces the risk of defaults. Indeed, during the recent economic recovery, junk has been one of the hottest bond categories. Lately, however, the yield spread between Treasuries and junk funds has been about 3.5 points, the low end of their range. So high-yield issues don't have as much room to recreate the glory days of recent years. Junk fund managers predict a still respectable return as long as the recovery stays on track and yields on competing investment-quality bonds don't spike up further.

Tax-exempt municipals. These funds buy bonds issued by cities, states and other local government entities. Also known as municipal bond funds, all of them produce dividends free of federal income tax. The dividends from so-called single-state muni funds, which invest entirely within the borders of one state, are exempt from state and local taxes as well for resident shareholders. Muni funds are most appealing to people in the 28% federal tax bracket and above. To learn how to calculate the taxable equivalent for any muni yield, complete the worksheet "Figuring What Muni Funds Pay" at right.

Analysts say that a growing appetite for tax-frees and a shrinking supply also bodes well for muni prices. One reason is that aging baby boomers will increasingly need

Figuring What Muni Funds Pay

With today's higher tax rates, tax-free investments have become even more appealing. This worksheet, illustrated with the example of a Philadelphia resident who pays federal tax at the 28% rate, state tax at 2.8% and city tax at 4.96%, will show you how much a taxable investment would have to pay you to match the after-tax yield of a bond or fund paying a triple-tax-free 4.9%. (If you pay no city income tax, enter zero in the appropriate space in step one.) As the result in step five demonstrates, a fully taxable fund would have to yield at least 7.4% to net more after-tax income than the triple-tax-free choice.

1. Total your state and city tax rates, expressed as a decimal number.

	+		=	
0.028 (Pa.)	+	0.0496 (Philadelphia)	=	0.0776

2. Multiply the result by 1 minus your federal tax rate.

	x	(1-)	=	
0.0776	x	(1-0.28)	=	0.0559

3. Add the result to your federal tax rate.

	+		=	
0.0559	+	0.28	=	0.3359

4. Subtract the sum from 1.

1-	=	
1-0.3359	=	0.6641

5. Divide the result into the tax-free yield, expressed as a decimal.

	÷		=	
0.049	÷	0.6641	=	0.0738

to save on a tax-sheltered basis. Another: hundreds of billions of dollars' worth of bonds have been taken off the market as municipalities retired the high-income bonds they issued in the early 1980s. But you still need to be cautious. Unless otherwise stated in the prospectus, most muni funds tend to hold longer-term securities than comparable corporate or government funds, making the muni funds more sensitive to interest-rate fluctuations. Also check the fund's annual report to make sure that it isn't trying to pump up yield by loading up on the offerings of frequently shaky muni issuers like industrial development agencies or hospitals. Analysts say that the slight increase in yield (normally three-tenths of a percentage point or so) just isn't worth the considerably greater default risk.

If you're considering a single-state fund, you must carefully weigh its credit risk. In the event your state runs into budget problems, the fund has nowhere to hide. As a result, your shares could be hammered. So if a single-stater makes sense for you, stick with funds in which interest and dividend payments are backed by commercial bond insurers. Even then, the fund should offer an after-tax yield advantage of at least half a percentage point over comparable national munis to justify the extra risk.

Foreign bonds. Diversification is the main reason to invest a portion of your fixed-income portfolio overseas. As in stocks, international diversification in bonds can reduce risk and enhance long-term gains. That's because the U.S. and foreign bond markets rarely move in unison. When one is down, the other is often rising. Remember, however, that foreign bond funds face the same currency risks discussed in the previous chapter. When you invest in foreign securities of any kind you run the risk that a rising dollar will shrink their value. Most international bond funds try to minimize such risks by using hedging techniques in the foreign exchange markets. The most common is dollar hedging, in which the global fund trades futures and options in overseas currencies to reduce the impact of currency moves relative to the dollar. If the dollar rises, dropping the value of your foreign bond holdings, the futures or options contracts theoretically rise in value to offset those decreases. The second form of currency defense is cross hedging, in which funds buy offsetting positions in different foreign currencies to soften the effect of fluctuations.

Neither form of hedging is an unmitigated plus. Buying options or protective positions can be expensive, shaving your fund's profits by as much as 5%. And fund managers can guess wrong about shifts in exchange rates. Thus investors with long time frames generally are better off buying world income funds with a policy of riding out currency swings, which experts say tend to equalize over periods of five to 10 years.

 ## Hybrids for Hearty Total Returns

What's wrong with this picture? Consider that roughly 75% of bond fund investors don't spend a penny of the income their funds produce. Instead, they reinvest their payout in more fund shares, suggesting many mistakenly use bond funds as tools for capital growth. Yet the bond market's historic return is only about half that of stocks. In other words, if you rely entirely on bonds to meet your long-range financial goals, you risk coming up short.

What about bonds' reputation for lower risk? Well, it's generally true, but not always. As interest rates zigzagged through the 1980s, long-term corporate and government bonds were nearly 20% more volatile than the S&P 500 index. Then you have to factor in the pernicious effect of inflation. Looking back at all the five-year periods since 1937 (meaning 1937 through 1941, 1938 through 1942, and so on), the stocks in the S&P 500 beat inflation by an average of 7.3 percentage points a year. But the typical intermediate-term Treasury bond nosed out rising prices by a meager 0.8 points.

So if you have financial goals that are more than five years off, take a deep breath and admit that at least some of your money belongs in stocks. That doesn't mean you have to dive into the deep end of the market where the aggressive growth funds swim, however. Instead, wade into total return funds, a moderate-risk catchall embracing such categories as equity income, growth and income, convertibles, balanced, flexible income and asset allocators. All aim for returns that blend the bondlike attributes of steady income (typically yielding 2% to 5%) with stocklike spurts of capital appreciation that averaged 9% to 13% annually in recent years. That has allowed them to grow several percentage points a year faster than bond funds while avoiding the unnerving volatility of racier stock funds.

Total return funds that go 40% or more into fixed-income securities, like the Income Fund of America, are about a third less volatile than those that traditionally keep 85% or more of their portfolios in stocks, like Massachusetts Investors Trust. Such stock-heavy total return funds are about 25% less topsy-turvy than pure growth funds. A total return fund's subcategory can give a quick insight as to where it fits on the bonds/stocks continuum. Flexible-income funds, for example, rely most heavily on bonds, typically holding just 20% of their assets in stocks. Convertible securities funds store at least 60% of their money in bonds or other fixed-income choices that can be traded in for shares of common stock. The trade-off: convertibles typically yield one to three percentage points less than straight corporate bonds while offering at least half the potential capital appreciation of the issuer's common stock. Balanced funds aim for a roughly 60-40 split between stocks and bonds, compared with about 75-25 for equity income portfolios. So-called growth and income funds, which tend to be at least 80% invested in stocks, are the group's most market-driven entries.

If you're considering total return funds that keep more than 20% of their assets in bonds, call the fund and request figures on its bonds' *average weighted maturity* and *credit quality*. As explained earlier in this chapter, short-term and intermediate issues hold their value far better than bonds with maturities of 10 years or more when interest rates rise. Credit quality is a concern on securities rated below investment grade (BB or lower from Standard & Poor's or Baa or lower from Moody's). The greater the proportion of suspect IOUs, the more susceptible the fund is to losses when the economy slows and issuers struggle to pay interest.

✦ Four

Choosing the Best Fund Family

What are the most telling traits that often distinguish great fund families—those one-stop emporia of stock, bond and money-market portfolios sponsored by a single investment company? It all depends on the family values you prize most as an investor. Above-average returns? Superior customer service? Low fees?

MONEY has the answers. Most people know that the fund business has long been dominated by Fidelity, whose 172 funds lately had combined assets of $250 billion, almost $100 billion more than the nearest competitor. Our study shows that Fidelity also ranks No. 1 overall in performance, the statistic that matters most to investors. In fact, the Boston powerhouse took three of the top six places in our exclusive ranking of the 25 biggest full-service fund houses and two discount brokerages that operate large no-load fund networks.

Money Ranks 27 Dynasties

Placing first was the $10 billion Fidelity Advisor series, which manages 16 funds sold through brokers and banks, followed by the $240 billion Fidelity retail group, which runs 156 funds sold directly to investors. Finishing sixth was Fidelity FundsNetwork, part of a discount brokerage that markets 192 no-load funds (71 of them managed by its parent). That put the network well ahead of its only direct rival on our list, Charles Schwab's 249-fund OneSource, No. 20 in our ranking. In third, fourth and fifth place respectively were $90 billion American Funds (with 27 funds), $27 billion Oppenheimer (38 funds) and $49 billion Prudential (69 funds). For a complete breakdown of the results, refer to the tables that follow at the end of this chapter.

We designed our study to help investors choose among the thousands of stock and bond funds. True, such famous fund standouts as Acorn, CGM Capital Development, Lindner and Mutual Shares don't belong to major families. Nonetheless, there are sound reasons to choose funds in the strongest families. For one thing, it's easier than trying to judge every contender on its individual merits. "Investors want ways to narrow their search for a fund," says Don Phillips of Morningstar, the fund research service that helped us rank the families. "And a fund's family affiliation provides one." Moreover, investing in a family of funds offers great convenience. When you want to reallocate your portfolio, you can simply pick up the phone and switch from one fund to a stablemate, usually at no cost. While convenience doesn't register in performance rankings, it can make a difference in your return. "If keeping money at one fund family means that you'll implement a strategy rather than just think about it, then it's a good idea," says San Francisco money manager Steve Janachowski.

Which families deserve the most loyalty? To find out, we pitted the 25 largest full-service fund families and the two leading discount brokerages' no-load programs against each other. We included the discounters because, like traditional families, these plans let you trade any fund on their roster over the phone with no transaction fee and track your holdings on a single monthly statement. The crucial difference is that, unlike the traditional families, the discounters let you move money among funds from many different no-load groups. To qualify for our study, a fund group or brokerage fund network had to have at least one fund with a three-year record or longer in each of five general asset categories (growth, total return, overseas stocks, taxable bond and tax-exempt bond). These limitations excluded some well-known groups, including $8 billion Strong, $16 billion Janus and $26 billion Twentieth Century, all of which lack seasoned overseas funds. Still, the 25 families that qualified collectively manage 57% of all dollars in stock and bond funds.

We then asked Morningstar to compare the performance of each organization's funds with others of the same type according to their risk-adjusted return. This calculation rewards a fund for earning high returns with low volatility. A fund was rated on a scale of 1 to 100 (a so-called percentile ranking) over all three-year periods in which it existed. Morningstar then averaged each fund's various three-year percentiles to arrive at a single score for the fund. The scores of all the funds within an investment category were combined to produce an average for each of the five investment categories in a family. These scores, in turn, were averaged to come up with a single overall score for each family.

Our method introduced some biases. We gave each fund and fund category the same weight, regardless of the relative amounts of assets involved, to highlight families with a range of top performers. In addition, our methodology gave a slight advantage to newer funds. Reason: it's easier to sustain terrific risk-adjusted returns over a few three-year periods than over dozens. Even so, no family could show up well in our rankings without a consistent risk-adjusted performance across the full range of investment categories. However you measure it, that's a noteworthy achievement for investors to weigh.

Whose research has the winning edge? Critics of Fidelity sometimes accuse the firm of flooding the marketplace with funds to increase the chances that one Fidelity product or another will always top the performance charts. But in our ranking, the Fidelity Advisor and Fidelity funds stood out because of their remarkable consistency in all categories. The two families ranked 1 and 2, respectively, in the growth category, long a Fidelity specialty. In addition, both Fidelity families scored above the median in the four other asset categories, placing among the top five in three of them (growth, taxable bond and municipal bond). Fidelity also finished in the top five for total return funds, giving the company four top-five results, a feat matched only by $10 billion Phoenix. The table on the right highlights the top performers within each of our investment groups.

Fund specialists such as Sheldon Jacobs of the newsletter *No-Load Fund Investor* attribute Fidelity's strong performance to the company's research department, whose legions of stock and bond analysts serve as a kind of farm team of future managers. Standout researchers get a chance to manage a single-industry sector fund. If they continue to do well, they may graduate to running one of the firm's diversified portfolios. Because most Fidelity managers have followed much the same career path and typically have worked together as analysts or junior portfolio managers, many funds have developed an informal team-management style. One result is that Fidelity funds often end up owning many of the same securities, which can magnify both successes and failures for the family as a whole.

Of the two discount brokerage fund networks, which charge no transaction fees, the Fidelity FundsNetwork owes its superior ranking mainly to the fact that it offers 71 Fidelity funds. Schwab's OneSource plan has none. (The Schwab network offers a number of mid-size families that recently were not available through Fidelity, including Montgomery, Twentieth Century and Warburg Pincus.) Like the Fidelity family, FundsNetwork showed strength in growth and taxable bond funds. But its

Top-Performing Clans by Category

GROWTH FUNDS	AVG. PERCENTILE
1. Fidelity Advisor	81
2. Fidelity	75
3. Prudential	69
4. Putnam	67
5. Phoenix	64

TOTAL RETURN FUNDS	AVG. PERCENTILE
1. Fidelity	76
2. Phoenix	76
3. American	74
4. Kemper	74
5. Prudential	70

OVERSEAS FUNDS	AVG. PERCENTILE
1. American	89
2. Dreyfus	89
3. Oppenheimer	87
4. Putnam	85
5. Franklin/Templeton	81

TAXABLE BOND FUNDS	AVG. PERCENTILE
1. USAA	67
2. Fidelity Advisor	66
3. Phoenix	63
4. Oppenheimer	62
5. Fidelity	61

MUNICIPAL BOND FUNDS	AVG. PERCENTILE
1. Alliance Capital	76
2. Fidelity Advisor	73
3. Prudential	68
4. Phoenix	65
5. Fidelity	61

strongest category was overseas funds. The network's international score exceeded that of the Fidelity family mainly because the network's smaller sample of overseas funds excludes some of the clan's lagging performers.

Who pays the bill for Fidelity's and Schwab's no-fee networks, since you don't? The funds do. The brokers charge each fund sponsor about a quarter of one percent of the assets held through their accounts annually. The fund companies accept the tariff because they believe the brokers help attract new investors. Some experts predict, however, that the participating fund companies will try to recoup the added cost by passing it on to the consumer in the form of higher expense ratios.

Which firms give investors the best service?

After returns, what you expect most from a fund is flaw-less record keeping, convenient switching privileges among funds in the group, and ready access to information about your account and fund. According to various surveys, investors are generally quite satisfied with the service they receive from their funds. In particular, most fund groups appear to have mastered the science of keeping track of shareholder accounts. A MONEY poll found that few complained of inaccuracies in such basic services as crediting new investments.

Fund families give shareholders varying degrees of freedom to switch money from one fund to another. Some groups, including Fidelity and Vanguard, limit the number of exchanges you can make in a year. Others, including the two discount brokerages, discourage short-term trading by requiring that you own shares for six months before qualifying for unlimited free exchanges. Most fund groups permit transactions only during busi-ness hours, though at many groups the day is 12 hours or longer. Dreyfus, Fidelity, Fidelity FundsNetwork and Schwab's OneSource go even further with service repre-sentatives on hand 24 hours a day to take buy or sell orders. Seven companies (Invesco, Oppenheimer, T. Rowe Price, Scudder, Vanguard and the two discount brokerage plans) let you trade at any time over an automated phone system. Almost all the other fund families allow you to check fund prices or account balances around the clock with a Touch-Tone phone.

Fund groups differ in the quality of the information that they provide their shareholders. Our yardstick is Morningstar's shareholder report grade, an evaluation of every company's literature for clarity, frequency and openness. (The two brokerage networks do not issue their own prospectuses and annual reports.)

How do expenses add up? Fund costs come in two
forms (explained in detail in Chapter 5). Sales charges, extracted one way or another by every broker-sold fund and by some direct-sold funds as well, can be avoided by investing in no-loads. But all funds charge annual fees for management and administration. The majority of families in our study are sold by brokers who charge commissions of as much as 6.5% when you buy or sell shares. About half a dozen offer you the option instead of paying a so-called level load, which is lower than the normal front-end or back-end sales charge but is accompanied by higher annual expenses. One reason load funds dominate our rankings is that the brokers or financial advisers who sell them want to offer clients a full range of investment options. By contrast, no-load fund families, which sell directly to the public, often specialize in a single investment arena.

The $130 billion Vanguard family has by far the lowest expenses. Shareholders benefit from the group's unique corporate structure, in which the funds own the management company. That allows Vanguard to provide management and administrative services to the funds at cost. (At virtually every other family, the sponsor aims to make a profit at managing and administering the fund.) The result: Vanguard stock funds nick shareholders for only 0.4% of assets a year, on average, compared with an industry average of 1.4%. Vanguard bond fund holders pay just 0.2%, compared with a norm of 0.8%. After Vanguard, the most cost-efficient fund families turned out to be American for stock funds and USAA for bonds.

Comparing Family Values

Spearheaded by its standout growth funds, Fidelity dominates our ranking of 27 full-service fund families and discount brokerages with no-load fund networks. Fidelity Advisor, the firm's family of broker-sold funds, ranks first with an overall percentile score of 68—meaning that the average Fidelity Advisor fund outscored 68% of its closest peers. The Fidelity funds sold directly to shareholders placed second with a score of 65. And Fidelity FundsNetwork, an arm of the group's discount brokerage that sells funds without transaction fees, scored 59 to come in sixth.

To arrive at overall scores, we first averaged the rankings of a group's funds within their respective investment categories. For example, No. 4 Oppenheimer's overseas funds scored a remarkable 87, on average, while the firm's average domestic growth fund earned only a 37. Combining those scores with the other three categories and averaging the total, we arrived at Oppenheimer's overall score of 59. Convenience and cost also matter. No. 8 Dreyfus, for example, accepts orders 24 hours a day. But its stock and bond funds carry annual expenses averaging, respectively, 0.9% and 0.8% of assets. By contrast, rival Vanguard's phone reps are on duty only from 8 a.m. to 9 p.m. eastern time, Monday through Friday. But the firm's stock and bond funds carry annual expenses averaging just 0.4% and 0.2%. In addition, fund ranker Morningstar awards Vanguard's annual reports an A- for frankness and clarity, while Dreyfus' rate no better than C.

Notes: (d): Max. deferred sales charge N.A.: Not applicable [1]Except Select Funds (unlimited exchanges for $7.50 each; 0.75% redemption fee if held for less than 30 days), Internationals (free, unlimited exchanges, except for Southeast Asia, Emerging Markets and Latin America, which charge 1.5% redemption fee if held less than 90 days) and Spartan ($5 per exchange); fees waived for exchanges using automated phone system [2]Free, unlimited exchanges with automated phone system [3]Unlimited, free exchanges for funds held six months or more [4]Sales load charged if shares held less than six months [5]Round-trip exchanges [6]Sales load charged if shares held less than 30 days [7]Per fund [8]Transaction fee charged if short-term trades exceed four per year [9]Sat. 10 to 2 [10]Sat. 10 to 4 [11]Sat. 10 to 2 [12]Sat. and Sun. 9 to 5 [13]Exchanges by mail only [14]Hours for Mon. to Thurs.; Fri.: 7 a.m. to 10 p.m.; Sat.: 8 a.m. to 5 p.m.; Sun.: 6 p.m. to midnight [15]8.24% max. on contractual funds [16]9.00% max. on contractual funds [17]Templeton phone: 800-237-0738
Sources: Morningstar Inc., Chicago, Illinois, 800-820-8082; the funds.

PERFORMANCE ANALYSIS

FUND FAMILY (number of funds)	Overall score	Growth	Total Return	Overseas	Taxable Bond	Tax-exempt Bond
Fidelity Advisor (16)	68	81	64	58	66	73
Fidelity (156)	65	75	76	51	61	61
American (27)	60	58	74	89	56	21
Oppenheimer (38)	59	37	59	87	62	51
Prudential (69)	59	69	70	48	40	68
Fidelity FundsNetwork (192)	59	62	59	72	54	47
Putnam (77)	58	67	52	85	40	45
Dreyfus (136)	58	41	59	89	50	50
Franklin/Templeton(97)	57	64	58	81	31	53
Phoenix (17)	57	64	76	18	63	65
Kemper (59)	55	56	74	70	29	47
Alliance Capital (50)	55	62	59	47	31	76
Scudder (40)	53	40	47	75	53	49
T. Rowe Price (56)	53	54	56	57	53	44
Vanguard (75)	49	30	49	63	53	48
MFS (50)	48	38	66	64	31	45
USAA (26)	47	20	55	36	67	60
Merrill Lynch (203)	47	42	48	52	45	49
IDS (36)	46	43	70	42	43	29
Schwab OneSource (249)	45	58	52	37	42	38
United (16)	44	36	39	73	20	51
Lord Abbett (22)	39	42	43	25	41	46
Dean Witter (40)	39	35	37	75	31	16
Colonial (36)	37	27	61	12	41	45
Invesco (30)	37	40	60	33	33	18
Smith Barney Shearson (48)	36	43	59	20	24	35
PaineWebber (25)	34	34	19	40	32	43

Comparing Family Values

COMPANY PROFILE

FUND FAMILY (number of funds)	Best funds Stocks	Bonds
Fidelity Advisor (16)	Income & Growth	High-Income Muni
Fidelity (156)	Equity-Income II	Spartan High-Income
American (27)	Smallcap World	High-Income
Oppenheimer (38)	Main Street Income & Growth A	Strategic Income A
Prudential (69)	Equity-Income A	Structured Maturity A
Fidelity FundsNetwork (192)	Fidelity Equity-Income II	Spartan High-Income
Putnam (77)	New Opportunities A	Municipal Income A
Dreyfus (136)	Peoples Index	Short-Intermediate Muni
Franklin/Templeton(97)	Balance Sheet Investment	High-Yield Tax-Free
Phoenix (17)	Capital Appreciation	Multi-Sector Fixed A
Kemper (59)	Retirement II	Municipal Bond
Alliance Capital (50)	Growth A	Muni Income National A
Scudder (40)	Japan	Medium-Term Tax-Free
T. Rowe Price (56)	New Asia	Spectrum Income
Vanguard (75)	Asset Allocation	Municipal Limited-Term
MFS (50)	World Total Return A	Municipal High-Income A
USAA (26)	Mutual Income Stock	Tax-Exempt Short-Term
Merrill Lynch (203)	Global Allocation A	Muni Limited Maturity A
IDS (36)	Diversified Equity-Income	High-Yield Tax-Exempt
Schwab OneSource (249)	Evergreen Foundation	Strong Advantage
United (16)	Income	Municipal High-Income
Lord Abbett (22)	Equity 1990	Tax-Free Income National
Dean Witter (40)	Pacific Growth	Intermediate Income Secs.
Colonial (36)	Colonial A	U.S. Government A
Invesco (30)	Industrial Income	Tax-Free Long-Term Bond
Smith Barney Shearson (48)	Prin. Ret. 1998	Div. Strat. Inc. B
PaineWebber (25)	Growth A	Municipal High-Income A

SERVICE

FUND FAMILY (number of funds)	Number of free switches	Switching fee	Transaction hours (ET)	Morningstar shareholder report grade
Fidelity Advisor (16)	Unlimited	None	8:30 to 6	B-
Fidelity (156)	4 per year[1]	None	24 hours	B
American (27)	Unlimited	None	8 to 8	B
Oppenheimer (38)	None[2]	$5	8:30 to 8[9]	B-
Prudential (69)	Unlimited	None	8 to 6	C+
Fidelity FundsNetwork (192)	4 per year[3]	None[8]	24 hours	N.A.
Putnam (77)	Unlimited	None	8:30 to 8	B-
Dreyfus (136)	Unlimited	None	24 hours	C
Franklin/Templeton(97)	Unlimited[4]	None	8:30 to 8	C+
Phoenix (17)	Unlimited	None	8 to 4	C
Kemper (59)	Unlimited	None	8 to 7[10]	B
Alliance Capital (50)	Unlimited	None	9 to 4	B-
Scudder (40)	4 per year[5]	None	8 to 6[11]	B+
T. Rowe Price (56)	3 per year[5]	None	8 to 10[12]	A
Vanguard (75)	2 per year[5]	None	8 to 9	A-
MFS (50)	Unlimited	None	8 to 8	C+
USAA (26)	6 per year	None	9 to 9	B-
Merrill Lynch (203)	Unlimited	None	8:30 to 5:30	B+
IDS (36)	36 per year	None	8 to 6	C+
Schwab OneSource (249)	4 per year[3]	None[8]	24 hours	N.A.
United (16)	Unlimited	None	8 to 4:30[13]	B-
Lord Abbett (22)	Unlimited	None	9:30 to 4	C+
Dean Witter (40)	Unlimited[6]	None	Brokers only	C
Colonial (36)	Unlimited	None	8 to 8	C+
Invesco (30)	4 per year[7]	None	7 to midnight[14]	C
Smith Barney Shearson (48)	Unlimited	None	Brokers only	B
PaineWebber (25)	None	$5	9 to 4	C+

Comparing Family Values

EXPENSES

FUND FAMILY (number of funds)	% maximum sales load		Annual expenses (% of assets)		Phone (800)
	Stocks	Bonds	Stocks	Bonds	
Fidelity Advisor (16)	4.75	4.75	1.67	0.89	522-7297
Fidelity (156)	3.00[15]	0.40	1.49	0.66	544-8888
American (27)	5.75	4.75	0.86	0.86	421-0180
Oppenheimer (38)	5.75	5.00(d)	1.41	1.38	525-7048
Prudential (69)	5.25	5.00(d)	1.70	1.15	225-1852
Fidelity FundsNetwork (192)	None	None	1.27	0.69	544-9697
Putnam (77)	5.75	5.00(d)	1.48	1.14	225-1581
Dreyfus (136)	4.50	4.50	0.93	0.75	782-6620
Franklin/Templeton(97)	5.75[16]	4.50	1.01	0.69	342-5236[17]
Phoenix (17)	5.00(d)	4.75	1.48	0.95	243-4361
Kemper (59)	5.75	4.50	1.08	0.80	621-1048
Alliance Capital (50)	4.25	4.25	2.27	1.58	227-4618
Scudder (40)	None	None	1.42	0.84	225-2470
T. Rowe Price (56)	None	None	1.08	0.74	638-5660
Vanguard (75)	None	None	0.39	0.22	851-4999
MFS (50)	5.75	5.00(d)	1.58	1.27	225-2606
USAA (26)	None	None	1.13	0.45	531-8181
Merrill Lynch (203)	6.50	4.00	1.66	1.03	637-3863
IDS (36)	5.00	5.00	1.24	0.86	437-4332
Schwab OneSource (249)	None	None	1.28	0.76	266-5623
United (16)	5.75	5.75	0.98	0.69	366-5465
Lord Abbett (22)	5.75	4.75	1.34	0.54	874-3733
Dean Witter (40)	5.00(d)	5.50	1.95	0.89	869-3863
Colonial (36)	5.75	5.00(d)	1.75	1.19	525-8085
Invesco (30)	None	None	1.12	1.00	248-2828
Smith Barney Shearson (48)	5.00	4.50	1.90	1.22	221-8806
PaineWebber (25)	5.00(d)	5.00(d)	1.95	1.36	647-1568

◆ Five

Managing Your Funds Like a Pro

Investing, it's said, is the triumph of greed over fear. But greed has nothing to do with the need to buy your family a home, send your kids to college and fund your retirement. These are only some of the reasons why Americans put their money at risk in the securities markets. The day is long gone when you could expect to reach such goals on the meager proceeds of a money-market account or the eternally bullish advice of your broker. Mutual funds offer you a wealth of alternatives. For all the hype of their sponsors, funds do provide professional management at an affordable fee. In effect, they've made small investors big beneficiaries of Wall Street's expertise rather than the proverbial stooges on the losing end of the smart money's trades. That said, there's no guarantee a fund you fancy won't disappoint you as a result of its gold-plated sales charges, profligate overhead, poor investment decisions—or all of the above. The purpose of this final chapter is to supply you with a guide to taking the plunge as a fund investor without getting soaked, whether by marketers, the fund's management or the tax man.

Navigate the Maze of Marketers

No doubt you've found lots of folks eager for your business these days. There's that persistent broker who keeps calling and that smiling sales rep in your bank lobby. You may even encounter pitches for funds in such unlikely places as an airline seat, a utility bill or a newsletter from a professional organization. Here are tips on investing through brokers, banks, discount brokers, no-load families and affinity groups. Where you choose to buy should depend on how much guidance and convenience you demand. You should bear in mind, however, that hand-holders also hold out their hands. Personal advice and service will cost you more than doing the fund picking on your own.

Brokers for advice at a price. Investors who want advice typically turn to brokers and financial planners, who account for roughly 60% of mutual fund sales. But you have to pay for that service in the form of loads, or sales charges. These usually amount to 4% to 6% of your investment up front or a flat rate in the case of fee-only planners. There's nothing wrong with paying a load as long as the ongoing guidance and subsequent returns justify the cost. But avoid any broker or planner who pushes a fund without first learning about your financial situation, investment goals and tolerance for risk. And be sure to ask about the adviser's compensation for selling the fund. Some brokerages offer incentives for pushing the house brand.

No-load funds for independence. If you are willing to research funds on your own, it's probably a waste of money to pay a load and to miss out on the abundant no-load choices marketed directly by fund families. The first step is to write or call a fund group (most have toll-free numbers) and ask for a prospectus, an annual report and an application. You can arrange for telephone switching between funds, redemption by wire, check writing and other services. If you buy a fund on your own, of course, there is no one monitoring the account to stop you from making a mistake or to help you decide when to cut your losses or take a profit. Some no-load groups including Fidelity, Dreyfus and T. Rowe Price offer free retirement planning workbooks and assistance on asset allocation, however.

Discount brokers for one-stop shopping. Active investors who trade frequently may prefer to work with a discount broker, as explained in the previous chapter. A key attraction is the ability to buy and sell funds with a single phone call and without the hassle of multiple applications and other annoying paperwork.

Banks for convenience. Their target market tends to be beginning investors disappointed with returns on CDs or savings accounts. But think twice if you're tempted by higher yields. You are most likely to be offered a non-bank load fund from a limited range of sponsors or a bank-run fund that may be no bargain. None of these investments is insured by the Federal Deposit Insurance Corporation (FDIC). Remember too that the convenience of a bank can be oversold. Many bank-based brokers work for outside firms and move between branches, precluding the possibility of long-term stewardship of your money.

Affinity groups for variety. You may get a fund pitch from an organization you belong to or even a company you do business with. There are socially conscious funds with ethical buying criteria. And now corporations are muscling into the fund market. American Airlines pushes its no-load American AAdvantage money fund to passengers through inflight magazines and promotional cards on food trays. Don't rush to buy a fund simply because it is offered by a group that you know. For example, the American Association of Retired Persons puts its name on a group of funds managed by Scudder. These funds are just as good as, but no better than, others in Scudder's family. Investors should judge a fund not by its name or by who is peddling it but by its long-term track record.

 ## Get Tough on Insidious Fees

You can't really predict a fund's future returns from its past performance. But history is a very reliable guide to fund expenses, which play a crucial but often overlooked role in determining how much of your fund's gains actually wind up in your pocket. These fees include any sales charges you pay when buying or redeeming shares plus investment management fees and other administrative levies you are nicked for, year in and year out.

True, up-front sales charges have generally declined during the past decade, with few funds still extracting the maximum 8.5% levy. But management, marketing and administrative expenses have jumped big time. Annual fees for stock funds overall rose nearly 50% to 1.4% of assets over a recent 10-year period. For taxable bond funds, costs spurted 13% to 0.8%. Fund boosters claimed in the 1980s that fees would come down as fund size went up. Well, growth stock funds' assets lately were up 148% over a decade. But average annual expenses actually rose 30% to 1.3% of assets. Those hikes would have been easier to swallow in the 1980s, when stock funds gained an average of 14% a year and bond funds rose almost 13%. But high expenses can be a real drag in the slow-growth 1990s, when returns are expected to be closer to the historic norms of 10% for stocks and 7% for bonds. If stock returns fall back to 10%, expenses would eat up 15% of fundholders' returns, vs. just 7% in the 1980s.

To understand the impact of expenses, compare Ivy International and Harbor International, two similar funds managed by Hakan Castegren. The no-load Harbor, with its 1.2% expenses, rewarded investors with a recent five-year return that was two percentage points fatter per year than Ivy International's (partly because of Ivy's hefty 1.7% expenses). Investors in Ivy's most popular class A shares also paid a 5.75% initial sales charge. Carefully consider these and other fee-related issues:

Weigh the sales charge, or load.

You can avoid commissions altogether by buying your funds directly from a no-load family. That way, every dollar you invest will be working for you. If you choose to invest through a broker or financial planner, you'll most often be hit with a front load of 3% to 5% when you make your purchase. Beware of funds like Common Sense Growth and IDEX that grab 8.5% of assets. If your $10,000 investment returns 10% annually over 10 years, you'll wind up with $23,735 after suffering that 8.5% sales charge, $2,200 less than in a no-load posting the same return.

Newer on the scene are back loads, also known as contingent deferred sales charges. There's no fee to buy the fund. But you'll pay a stiff penalty if you cash out early, usually coughing up 1% to 5% of any withdrawal you make before the end of year five. A growing number of broker-sold fund groups, including Merrill Lynch, now offer you the choice of buying a fund with a front or back load. While choosing between these options may be confusing, experts say there's often little difference. That's because most back loads are accompanied by nettlesome 12b-1 fees (described in detail below), which boost annual expenses. You're probably best off paying a front load if you plan to hold your fund for just a few years and if the charge is 4.5% or less. Back loads tend to be more economical if your time horizon is five years or longer. While you're likely to pay a higher 12b-1 charge at the outset, in most cases it converts to a smaller service fee sometime between the seventh and ninth year.

Compare annual expense ratios.

That's your fund's costs as a percentage of its average net assets. You'll find this figure, plus a five-year expense projection, in the fee table near the front of every fund prospectus. You should generally avoid a fund if its fees are higher than the median for its investment objective (see the table "How Fund Fees Stack Up" on the next page for expense

How Fund Fees Stack Up

To ensure that you're not overpaying for a fund, you should compare its expense ratio with its category below. Why the discrepancy between categories? Fund experts explain that running, say, a small-cap growth portfolio is more manager-intensive and thus justifiably pricier.

Fund Objective	Median annual expenses	Lowest-highest annual expenses
Overseas stock	1.8 %	0.28 to 3.67 %
Aggressive growth	1.7	0.72 to 3.00
Small-company growth	1.4	0.18 to 3.12
Capital growth	1.3	0.30 to 3.10
High-yield bond	1.2	0.33 to 2.49
Growth and income	1.2	0.15 to 3.14
Investment-grade corp. bond	0.7	0.30 to 2.02
Long-term muni bond	0.8	0.14 to 2.57
Money market	0.8	0.25 to 1.61

benchmarks on nine key fund categories). If you're torn between two funds of the same type with comparable records, opt for the one with lower expenses.

Watch out for vexing 12b-1 fees. Named after a Securities and Exchange Commission rule, 12b-1 fees allow funds to recoup their advertising and marketing costs by skimming a bit from current shareholders. These charges now range from 0.1% to 1.25% of assets per year and are included in your fund's expense ratio.

Fund companies claim that 12b-1 fees actually benefit investors by allowing funds to gather more assets and thus spread their costs over a bigger base, reducing expenses. But a study by State University of New York (Buffalo) finance professor Charles Trczinka found that funds with 12b-1 fees don't seem to pass economies of scale along to their investors. A fairly new SEC rule, which was championed by the National Association of Securities Dealers, requires funds to include 12b-1 fees when calculating sales charges. The rule limits annual 12b-1 fees to 0.75% of net assets but allows funds to charge a 0.25% service fee. The measure also caps total sales charges including 12b-1 at 6.25% to 8.5%, depending upon the fund's fee schedule.

Factor in the cost of portfolio turnover. You might not think of turnover, or how often your fund trades its holdings, as a significant expense. But high turnover can cut into your returns. That's because the fund pays a brokerage commission on each trade and, in some cases, may actually move a stock's price with a buy or sell decision. Each time your fund turns over its entire portfolio (a 100% turnover rate), it costs you 0.5% to 1%, figures Trczinka. Thus he says a fund that has a 200% turnover rate could run you $200 for each $10,000 you've invested. In addition, you'll have to pay capital gains tax on your share of any profits the fund passes along to you (to avoid shelling out more than your due, be sure to consult "Trim Uncle Sam's Take" later in this chapter). Of course, taxed gains are better than no gains. Turnover may be an indication of appropriately active and vigilant management, particularly in the more volatile fund categories such as aggressive and small-company growth.

 ## Don't Overlook the Prospectus

Whenever you come across some promising funds, take the time to phone each one to request its prospectus and most recent annual and quarterly reports. (Most funds include an application form with these documents.) Or, in the case of a load fund, you can get these documents from your broker or financial planner.

Although a fund's prospectus is by design a dull read, it is full of useful facts and disclosures required by federal securities law. In general, a prospectus describes the fund's investment objectives, strategies and risks; presents statistics on its past performance; lists the sales and management fees; and explains how you can buy and sell shares. Make sure that you are sent a copy of the prospectus' statement of additional information, usually referred to as Part B. This document is particularly important because it describes in detail a mutual fund's complete fee structure, a subject that may be treated cursorily in the prospectus.

The cover of the prospectus lists the fund's address and phone numbers, and in most cases briefly summarizes the fund's objectives and states the initial sales charge, if any. Though formats vary, most prospectuses are divided into a dozen or so sections. Start your examination with the section commonly called "General Description of the Fund." Ranging in length from a few paragraphs to more than a page, this section should spell out the difference between the fund's objectives and its policies (i.e., the investment strategies and techniques it is permitted to employ to achieve its objectives). These might include buying stocks on margin (using money borrowed from brokers), trading stock options or other sophisticated tactics you may not feel comfortable with.

Pay particular attention to the table usually called "Per-Share Data." This table gives the fund's annual performance over the past 10 years, or the life of the fund if it is younger than that. It shows you whether a fund's performance has been steady or erratic, and it can be used to compare a fund's year-to-year changes in share value with those of other funds with similar objectives. For example, does the fund owe much of its long-term return to one or two lucky years, or did it consistently outperform comparable funds and market barometers such as the S&P 500 index? Investors should also take the time to scan through sections titled "How to Purchase Shares" and "How to Redeem Shares" that explain the mechanics of getting into and out of the fund, whether by mail, phone or wire. They also tell you whether there is a sales charge; a minimum initial investment or a minimum for subsequent investments; a fee for switching from one fund in the same family to another; or a charge that may be levied for redeeming your shares.

Check Out the Fund Manager

When you put money in a fund, you aren't just acquiring shares in a portfolio of stocks or bonds. You are also paying for topnotch management—or so you hope. Thus, before committing your cash, you should learn as much as possible about the person or persons making the fund's day-to-day investment decisions. Managers come and go, and the hotshot stock picker who propelled a fund to the top of the performance charts last year may have long since left. So unless you know from reading newspapers and magazines that your fund is run by a widely respected portfolio manager, you'll want to delve into the following issues concerning the manager, whom we will refer to as Jones.

How long has Jones run the show? For all the data disclosed in a fund's prospectus and shareholder reports, you won't necessarily find the portfolio manager's name listed in these documents. But you can often learn it and how long he or she has been in charge by calling the fund. Some won't tell you because they don't want to tie their reputations to that of an individual who might leave, causing investors to pull out their money. In that case, you usually can find the manager's name and tenure in references, such as Morningstar's, available at many libraries. Then compare the manager's tenure with the fund's performance. Check whether the manager has been at the helm since 1990, and thus in charge during the sharp market downturn in the summer of that year as well as the bull market that began in October 1990. If so, you can probably assume that the record shows the range of the manager's investing talents. If the manager came to the fund after 1990, those skills may not have been tested in tough times.

How crucial is Jones to your returns? This will depend largely on the fund's objectives, size and the way in which it is operated. For example, some funds have no single manager but are run instead by committees of analysts. With these funds, you should focus your attention on the team leader, if one is so designated. In general, funds that aim for aggressive growth are more apt to rely on the insights and skills of a single manager than are more conservative stock and bond portfolios. That's because aggressive growth funds typically try to take quick advantage of stock market movements and to invest in up-and-coming companies before their growth is obvious on Wall Street. To excel with this approach, a manager can't afford to wait for a cumbersome investment committee to discuss and approve which stocks the fund should buy or sell. Instead, the fund needs a decisive manager who has uncommonly good judgment and instincts. Conversely, individual expertise matters less if the fund's strategy is to invest narrowly in certain types of bonds or in specific industries. Most specialty funds stick to stocks in their particular sector, such as electric utilities or health care providers. So their fortunes fluctuate largely in step with those of their industry no matter how talented the manager is.

How should you react if Jones leaves? Whether you too should consider jumping ship will depend on how much influence Jones had and the fund's relative returns prior and subsequent to his or her departure. If the value of your fund starts to sink, while the market is buoyant, you will obviously want to reevaluate your rationale for this particular investment.

Attend to Account Details

Opening a fund account is as easy as establishing a savings account at your local bank. Some funds will even let you open an account by phone if you have money in another fund in the same family and promise to send in your check promptly. Most fund applications consist of a single sheet of paper on which you supply such basic background information as your name, address, Social Security number (or taxpayer identification number) and birth date. You will be asked whether you want to open the account as an individual, which gives you alone the power to authorize switches and redemptions, or jointly with a spouse or friend. In that case, you or your co-owner can make investments on your own. But you both will have to sign all requests for redemptions and transfers of money to another fund. If you choose joint ownership, remember that in the event one of you dies, the other automatically owns all of the shares. If you buy them with someone else and leave your interest in the fund to a third person, you should instruct the fund on the application to register you and your co-owner as tenants in common. That way, if you die, the fund will transfer your rights in the fund to your designated beneficiary.

Setting up a distribution plan. Most funds require you to specify in advance what you want done with the capital gains realized in the portfolio plus the dividends and interest it generates. You have three choices. One, you can reinvest all distributions in the fund, adding to the number of shares you own. Two, you can have dividends paid to you in cash and capital gains distributions reinvested in additional shares. Or three, you can have both dividends and capital gains paid to you in cash. Unless you are an income investor, reinvestment of all distributions is probably your best choice because the newly purchased shares then begin generating capital gains and dividends. Whatever you decide, you will owe federal taxes on the distributions unless your shares are in a tax-exempt municipal bond fund or a tax-deferred account such as an IRA. (Note that capital gains earned by muni funds are subject to federal taxes; the interest income is not.)

Buying your fund shares. The price you pay is the fund's net asset value per share on the day the fund receives your application. You will not receive share certificates upon investing unless you request them. There is no reason you need them unless you plan to use them as collateral for a loan. In fact, having the certificates in your possession can be an inconvenience since you will not be able to switch money to another fund or redeem shares by phone. To purchase the most shares for your money, be mindful of the date you bought them. You are better off buying shares on the day after a fund declares its dividends ("goes ex-dividend" in investment parlance). Since such payments reduce the fund's NAV, the price of shares drops by that amount.

The value of your investment technically remains the same; you neither lose nor gain because each share is worth less than before the fund went ex-dividend. But by buying in after the dividend is declared, you will avoid having to pay taxes on that particular payout. Call the fund for the dates on which it goes ex-dividend. You also can tell when a fund has declared its payout by checking the fund listings in newspaper financial pages. Usually on the day after a dividend payment has been announced, an **x** appears beside the fund's NAV.

 ## Recognize When to Bail Out

Deciding when to sell a fund is among the most difficult tasks of investing. It's easy to be rational in evaluating a fund before you buy it. But once your money is committed, your emotions come into play, alternately tempting you to hold on to winners long after they have peaked and to jettison losers just before they bounce back. To spot the right time to sell or switch to another fund, you must continually compare the ones you own with others and with your personal financial goals. As long as your fund is meeting your objectives, you should hold on to it. But you shouldn't hesitate to move your money if another fund seems likely to do the job better. Financial advisers say you should consider selling or switching under each of the following circumstances.

When your financial situation changes. As you get older or closer to your goals, your needs and your tolerance for risk should change. When your children near college age, for example, you should stop taking risks with your investments for their tuition because you can't afford to lose a chunk of it in a last-minute market dip. When they are in high school you should begin switching some of the college money from growth funds to short-term bond and money funds.

When the fund itself changes. Try to think back to the reasons that initially led you to invest in a fund. If it no longer fits those criteria, you should consider looking for a replacement. For example, your growth fund's assets may have grown so large that you fear the manager has lost the flexibility that helped him or her get high returns. Or your fund may have increased its annual fees beyond what you are willing to pay. You might also decide to switch if the manager responsible for the fund's past success retires or quits. Fund groups may not be in a hurry to notify investors that the manager has left. But if you notice changes in performance, volatility or the fund's investment style, a new hand may be at the helm. To find out for sure, ask the fund.

When returns lag those of similar funds. If a fund turns out to be a subpar performer, you obviously will want to replace it. Sheldon Jacobs of the newsletter *No-Load Fund Investor* suggests you give a fund at least a year to prove itself. If you are in a conservative total return fund, he adds, you might even give it two years. "Some awfully good conservative funds can drop below the averages occasionally," he says. "You have to be patient." After two years, however, it's time to take your money out of the fund if it still languishes relative to its group or benchmarks like the S&P 500 index.

 ## Trim Uncle Sam's Take

Mutual funds are renowned for simplifying investors' lives—except at tax time. That's partly because tax law requires funds to pay out, or distribute, virtually all their income from interest, dividends and net capital gains each year. That means you often owe taxes on capital gains from your fund even if you didn't sell any shares. In fact, you may owe taxes even if you didn't make any money. That happened to shareholders of USAA Mutual Aggressive Growth in 1992. Although the fund shed nearly 9% of its value that year, it paid out $2.14 per share in taxable capital gains distributions because it unloaded some holdings at a profit during the year.

Things get more confounding when you do sell shares. If you're like most investors, you have your funds reinvest your distributions. From a tax standpoint, each reinvestment counts as a separate purchase. Thus you're confronted with a mess when you sit down to calculate your taxable gains. Included might be a large clump of shares you bought at one price (your initial investment); dozens of tiny lots acquired at different prices (shares purchased with reinvested distributions); and a further raft of small chunks each bought at yet another price (the regular purchases you made). Each lot of fund shares that you bought produces a different capital gain or loss, which means that much extra calculator punching to figure out what you owe Uncle Sam. Here are tips that can spare you some headaches.

Don't buy fund shares at the wrong time. Most stock funds distribute capital gains once a year, and some funds pay out income quarterly. (To learn your fund's distribution dates, call its 800 number.) If you're contemplating a purchase close to a distribution date, don't act until after the date passes. Otherwise, you'll receive a taxable payout of all the capital gains or income the fund booked since its last payout even if you've owned your stake for only a week. In effect, the fund hands you back part of your principal in the form of a distribution. But now you owe tax on it.

Check gains and losses on the fund's books.

When you're considering whether to buy a fund, check the changes in net assets in the fund's annual report. The number to look for is the "change in unrealized appreciation on investments." That represents capital gains embedded in the fund's portfolio. When the fund sells its winners, those gains must be distributed to shareholders. To judge how big the payout could be, divide the unrealized appreciation by the fund's net assets. A result of more than 0.2 suggests that a walloping big payout is possible. While the potential for a big distribution shouldn't rule out a promising fund, it could decide a close call between competing funds. In contrast, realized losses are a plus. The fund can use prior losses to offset gains for as long as eight years.

Take advantage of your own losses. If one of

your funds is down for the year, consider selling it and taking the tax write-off. The loss can offset capital gains plus as much as $3,000 of other income. In fact, it often makes tax sense to move out of a losing no-load fund temporarily even if you still like its prospects. The Internal Revenue Service will disqualify the loss if you repurchase shares within 31 days. But nothing prevents you from hopping into a similar fund for a little longer than that and then switching back to your favorite.

Consider selling out in the same year. While you

don't want to overrule your investment sense just to streamline your taxes, here's something to think about. If you sell a fund's shares over a number of years, you have to keep records of each sale and decide which of the four IRS approved accounting methods (described below) yields the lowest tax. If you sell all at once, all four methods will give you the same tax. So you can use the simplest method, called *average cost, single category.* It allows you to figure the average cost of all your shares, regardless of when you bought them. And that work will be done for you if the fund you're selling belongs to one of the growing number of families that calculate tax costs for redeeming shareholders (among them Vanguard, T. Rowe Price, Putnam and IDS). Keep in mind, however, that if you're not unloading all your shares, the single category method may cost you more in taxes than the alternatives described below.

Figure the most tax-efficient method. Unless you

elect otherwise at the time you sell only some of your fund shares, the IRS assumes that the ones you sold first were the ones you bought first. That method is called *first in, first out.* It's fine if your fund has been a loser. But the oldest shares typically have the biggest gains. So they're the ones on which you're better off postponing taxes. You can do that using a method called *specific identification.* It permits you to sell whichever shares will minimize your taxes. For example, you might pick only shares on which you have a loss, thereby offsetting gains from a different investment.

The fourth method, *average cost, double category,* requires you to distinguish between shares that you've held for more than a year and those you bought more recently and to calculate a separate average cost for each. That way you can take advantage of the difference in tax rates on long-term and short-term gains. Long-term gains (on shares held more than a year) are taxed at a maximum of 28%. Short-term gains are taxed as ordinary income at rates as high as 39.6%.

Here's a final caveat. Once you decide to use either single or double category for a given fund, you're stuck with that method for the fund. You are not permitted to change the tax treatment without written permission from the IRS. And don't hold your breath waiting for that.

Glossary of Fundspeak

Aggressive growth fund. One that strives for maximum capital gains, as opposed to current income, from stocks of any size that are expected to appreciate faster than the market overall.

Asset allocation fund. Offers investors one-stop shopping for their portfolio requirements. These funds spread their assets among a variety of investments such as U.S. stocks, foreign stocks, precious metals and bonds, altering the mix in an effort to time the market and enhance shareholders' returns.

Back-end load. See **Redemption fees**.

Balanced fund. An income-oriented portfolio that typically has an even-handed mix of bonds and stocks (including convertible and preferred shares).

Bond. Interest-paying government or corporate security that obligates the issuer to pay the holder a specified sum, usually at specific intervals, and to repay the principal amount, or face value, of the bond at maturity.

Certificate of deposit (CD). Debt instrument, issued by financial institutions, that usually pays interest.

Closed-end fund. One with a limited number of shares outstanding. Unlike conventional open-end funds, which continually buy and sell their shares at net asset value, closed-end funds have a fixed number of shares that trade the way stocks do on exchanges or over the counter.

Compounding. Earnings on your investment's earnings. For example, if you've invested $1,000 earning 5% a year, after one year you'll have $1,050. During the second year, you will earn interest not only on the original $1,000, but also on the $50 in earnings. Over time, compounding can lead to significant growth in your investment.

Contingent deferred sales charge (CDSC). A fee imposed when shares are redeemed (sold back to the fund) during the first few years of share ownership. See also **Redemption fees**.

Convertible. Corporate bond or preferred stock that is exchangeable for a set number of common shares at a prestated price.

Credit rating. Evaluation of debt securities' credit risk, or likelihood of default, by rating services such as Moody's Investors Service and Standard & Poor's Corporation.

Diversification. The spreading of one's investment risk by putting assets in a wide-ranging portfolio of securities, such as a mutual fund.

Dividend. Distribution of earnings to shareholders. Fund dividends are paid out of income generated by stocks and bonds in the portfolio, usually on a quarterly basis.

Dollar cost averaging. An installment purchase technique that involves investing a fixed amount of money in stocks or mutual fund shares at regular intervals, such as monthly or quarterly, rather than all at once. The objective of the strategy is to buy fewer shares when prices are high and more shares when they are low.

Exchange privilege. An option enabling fund shareholders to transfer their investment from one fund to another within the same fund family, as their needs or objectives change. Funds typically allow investors to use the exchange privilege several times a year for free or for a low fee.

Ex-dividend. Period between the announcement and the payment of a mutual fund's next dividend. An investor who buys shares during that interval is not entitled to the dividend. A fund that has gone ex-dividend is marked with an "x" in newspaper listings.

Exit fee. See **Redemption fees**.

Expense ratio. Amount, expressed as a percentage of total assets, that shareholders paid in the past year for mutual fund operating expenses and management fees.

Front-end load. See **Load**.

Ginnie Mae. The nickname for the federally backed debt securities issued by the GNMA (Government National Mortgage Association). Ginnie Maes represent a pool of mortgages; investors receive the homeowners' payments of interest and principal.

Growth fund. One whose main objective is capital appreciation by investing in stocks that are expected to increase steadily in value over time.

Growth stock. Share in an expanding company that has reported above-average earnings gains over the last few years and is expected to maintain or increase its growth rate in the years ahead.

Hedge. A defensive investment strategy, often involving the buying or selling of options, to offset possible losses and thereby to reduce risk.

Income fund. A portfolio that is managed to generate steady income rather than capital gains by investing in bonds, high-dividend stocks and other income-producing securities.

Index fund. One whose portfolio closely duplicates that of an index such as the Standard & Poor's 500-stock index and whose performance therefore mirrors that of the market overall.

Individual Retirement Account (IRA). Personal retirement account that an employed person may be entitled to fund with tax-deductible contributions of up to $2000 per year ($2250 a year for a couple with a nonworking spouse). You can fully deduct your contribution if you are not covered by a pension plan or if you earn less than $25,000 (single) or $40,000 (married and filing jointly). All earnings generated in the account accumulate tax-deferred until the funds are withdrawn. Early withdrawals (those made before age 59.5) are subject to a 10% tax penalty and income taxes.

Junk bond. A high-yielding bond with a speculative credit rating (BB or lower grading, for example, by Standard & Poor's) that reflects doubts about the issuing company's or government's credit strength.

Load. Commission or sales charge for buying fund shares through a broker, financial planner or insurance agent. Some funds that sell directly to the public also charge loads. Funds that do not are called no-load funds.

Management fee. Charge against investor assets to cover the costs of managing the portfolio of a mutual fund. The fee is a fixed percentage of the fund's assets and is disclosed in the fund's prospectus.

Market timing. A strategy of buying or selling securities, including fund shares, to take advantage of (or reduce one's exposure to) anticipated changes in market conditions. For example, fund shareholders might switch from a stock fund to a short-term bond or money-market fund when they think the stock market is about to fall.

Maturity. The date on which a bond's principal becomes due and payable.

Money-market fund. One that invests in short-term government securities, bank certificates of deposit and other low-risk, low-return securities. These funds pay so-called money market rates of interest, and withdrawals from them can be made anytime at a predictable per-share value.

Municipal bond. Bond issued by a state or local government. In most cases, the interest paid is exempt from federal taxes and, if the bondholder lives in the state where the bond was issued, from state and local taxes too.

Mutual fund. An investment company that raises money from shareholders and invests it in stocks, bonds and other types of securities. Most mutual funds are open-ended, which means that they continuously sell new shares to investors and stand ready to buy back (redeem) shares at their net asset value. Funds offer investors the advantages of diversification, professional management and low transaction costs, in exchange for which they charge a modest management fee.

Net asset value (NAV). The value of a share of a mutual fund. A fund computes its NAV daily by taking the closing prices of securities in its portfolio, adding the value of other assets such as cash, subtracting the fund's liabilities, and dividing the result by the number of shares outstanding.

Operating expenses. The normal costs a mutual fund incurs in conducting business, such as the expenses associated with maintaining offices, staff and equipment. There are also expenses related to maintaining the fund's portfolio of securities. These expenses are paid from the fund's assets before any earnings are distributed to shareholders.

Option. An agreement that gives the buyer the right to buy (call option) or sell (put option) 100 shares of a particular stock or stock index at a fixed price during a preset period. An option produces income, called a premium, for the seller, who gives up ownership of the securities if the option buyer exercises his right.

PE. See **Price-earnings ratio**.

Portfolio turnover. A measure, usually expressed in annual terms, of how frequently a fund's manager trades in and out of the securities in the fund.

Preferred stock. A class of stock that pays a fixed dividend and has preference over common stock in the payment of dividends and the liquidation of the issuing company's assets. Preferred stockholders do not normally have voting rights.

Price-earnings ratio (PE). Also known as the earnings multiple, it gives investors an idea of how much they are paying for a stock's earnings or a fund's portfolio. The ratio is figured by dividing a stock's price by its earnings per share as reported over the past 12 months or forecast in future years by analysts who follow the company. The higher the PE, the higher the profit growth investors expect in the future.

Prospectus. The official document that a mutual fund supplies to all prospective shareholders, identifying the fund's management company, outlining its investment objectives and assessing the risks involved. A corollary document, called Part B or the statement of additional information, provides greater details on subjects such as fees.

Redeem. To cash in your shares by selling them back to the mutual fund. Shares may be redeemed on any business day.

Redemption fees. Often called exit fees or back-end loads, they are deducted from money you take out of some funds when you redeem, or sell, shares. Some exit fees, which can be as high as 1% of the amount redeemed, decline to zero over a period of a few months or years; others remain constant. Back-end loads, also known as contingent deferred sales charges, typically are levied by load funds that do not have initial, or front-end, sales charges. The loads start at 4% to 6% on withdrawals during your first year in the fund and gradually decline to zero over four to six years.

Reinvestment privilege. An option that's available to fund shareholders in which distributions of dividends and capital gains are automatically turned back into the fund to buy new shares and thus increase holdings.

Single-state muni fund. One specializing in tax-exempt bonds of government agencies within a single state. Residents of that state receive income from the bonds that is free from state as well as federal taxes.

Specialty fund. Also called a sector fund, it restricts its holdings to the stocks of companies in a particular industry, service or region. Specialty funds are often grouped into families, and investors switch among funds as economic and market conditions warrant.

Standard & Poor's 500-stock index. A popular measurement of the stock market's performance based on prices of 500 common stocks listed on the New York and American stock exchanges or traded over the counter.

Total return. The dividends, interest and capital gains that a fund achieves over a given period of time.

Total return fund. One that pursues both growth and income by investing in a mix of high-yielding stocks and bonds.

12b-1 fees. Named after a Securities and Exchange Commission rule that permits them, these assessments against shareholders' assets are levied by many mutual funds to help pay for promotion expenses. Such 12b-1 fees are usually included in a fund's expense ratio.

Volatility. The degree to which securities such as mutual fund shares move up or down in price within a given period.

Yield. The dividend or interest income that a stock, bond or mutual fund share pays out in one year, expressed as a percentage of the issue's price or the fund's net asset value.

Zero-coupon bond. A bond that makes no periodic interest payments but instead is sold at a discount from its face value. The buyer of a zero receives the rate of return by the gradual appreciation of the bond, which is redeemable at face value on its maturity date.

◆ Index